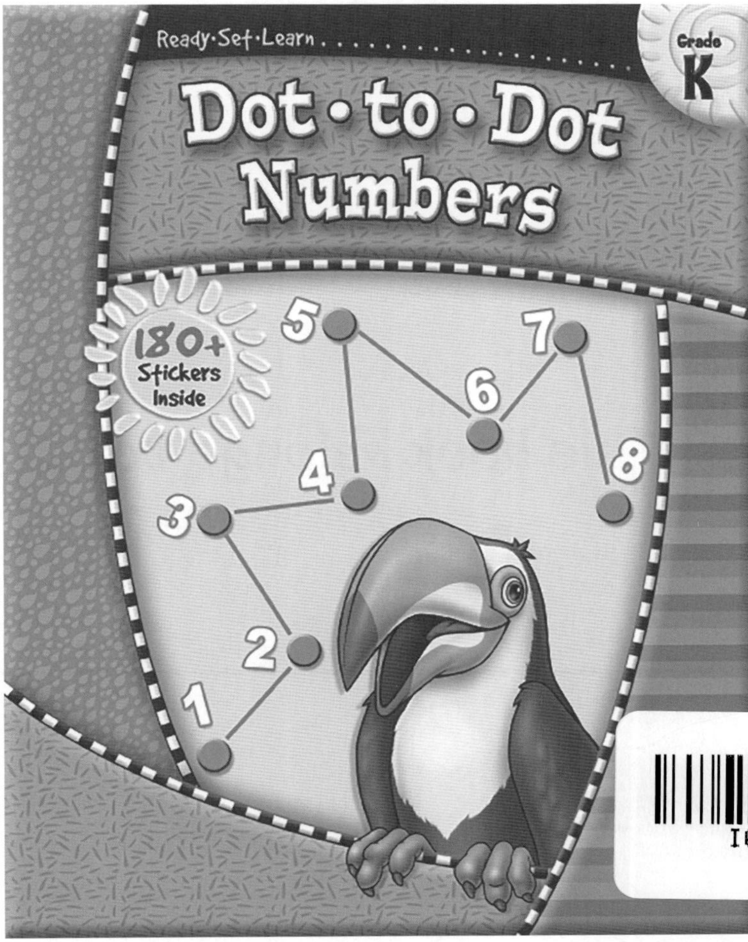




**Managing Editor**
Ina Massler Levin, M.A.

**Editor**
Eric Migliaccio

**Contributing Editor**
Sarah Smith

**Creative Director**
Karen J. Goldfluss, M.S. Ed.

**Cover Design**
Tony Carrillo / Marilyn Goldberg

**Teacher Created Resources**
12621 Western Avenue
Garden Grove, CA 92841
www.teachercreated.com

ISBN: 978-1-4206-5957-3



Reprinted, 2026 (PO606216)

Made in U.S.A.

Teacher Created Resources

This book belongs to

______________________

Ready·Set·Learn

# Get Ready to Learn!

Get ready, get set, and go! Boost your child's learning with this exciting series of books. Geared to help children practice and master many needed skills, the *Ready·Set·Learn* books are bursting with 64 pages of learning fun. Use these books for . . .

- enrichment
- skills reinforcement
- extra practice

With their smaller size, the *Ready·Set·Learn* books fit easily in children's hands, backpacks, and book bags. All your child needs to get started are pencils, crayons, and colored pencils.

A full sheet of colorful stickers is included. Use these stickers for . . .

- decorating pages
- rewarding outstanding effort
- keeping track of completed pages

Celebrate your child's progress by using these stickers on the reward chart located on the inside cover. The blue-ribbon sticker fits perfectly on the certificate on page 64.

With *Ready·Set·Learn* and a little encouragement, your child will be on the fast track to learning fun!

# Ribbons and Bows (1-10)

# Home Sweet Home (1-10)

# What Is Falling? (1-10)

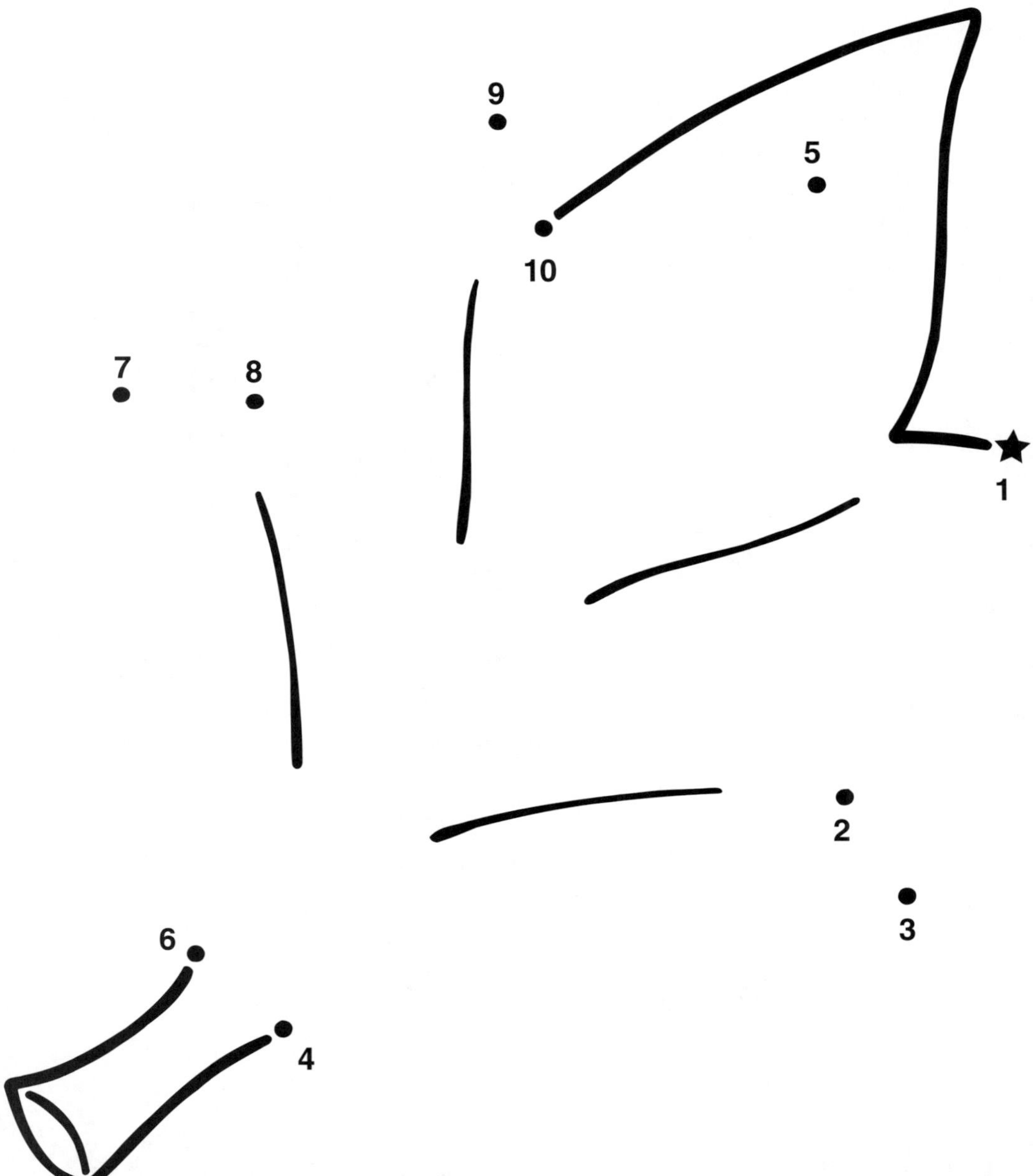

# Pencil (1-10)

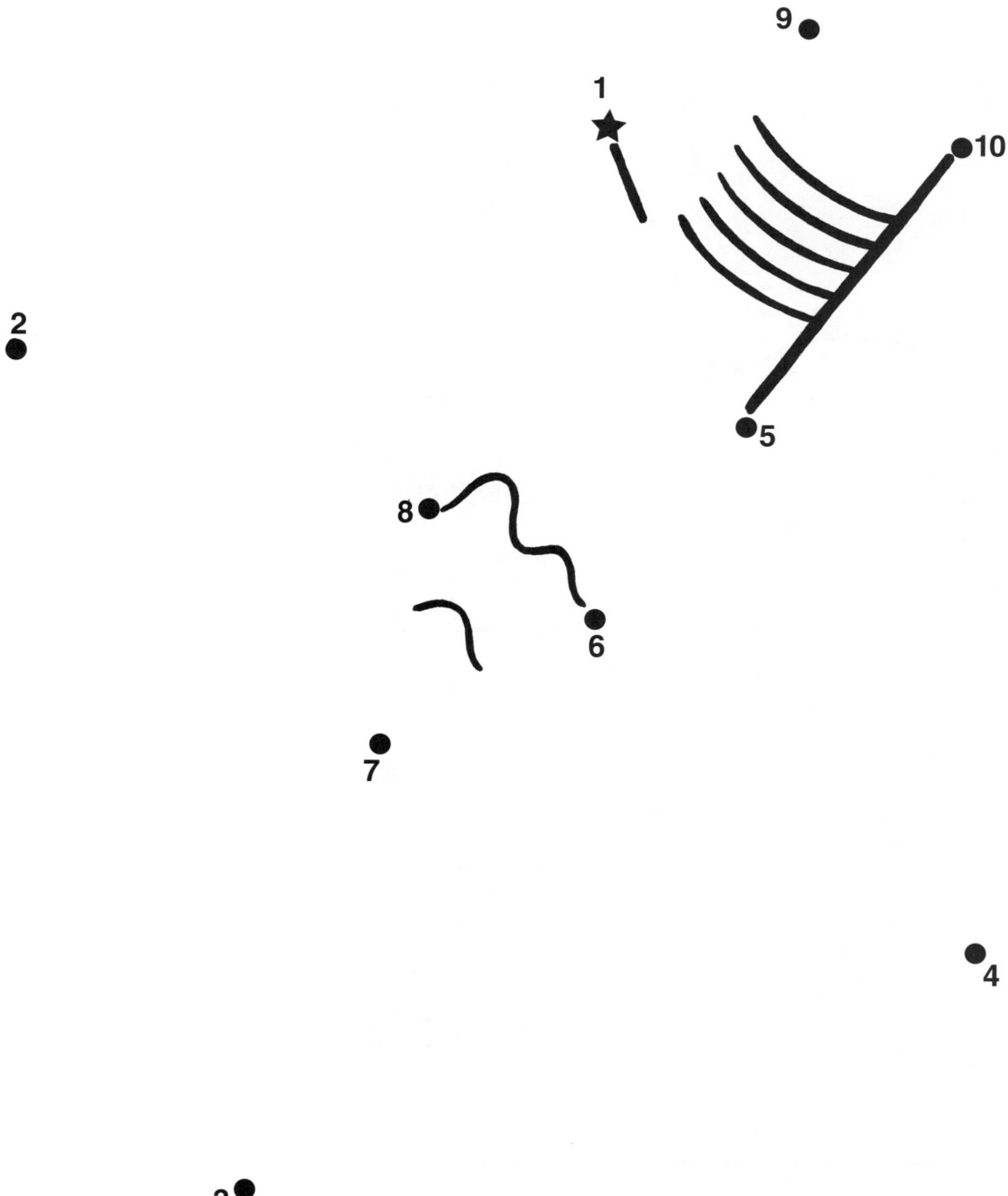

# Clown Face (1-10)

# Mmmm... (1-10)

# Mice and Cheese (1-10)

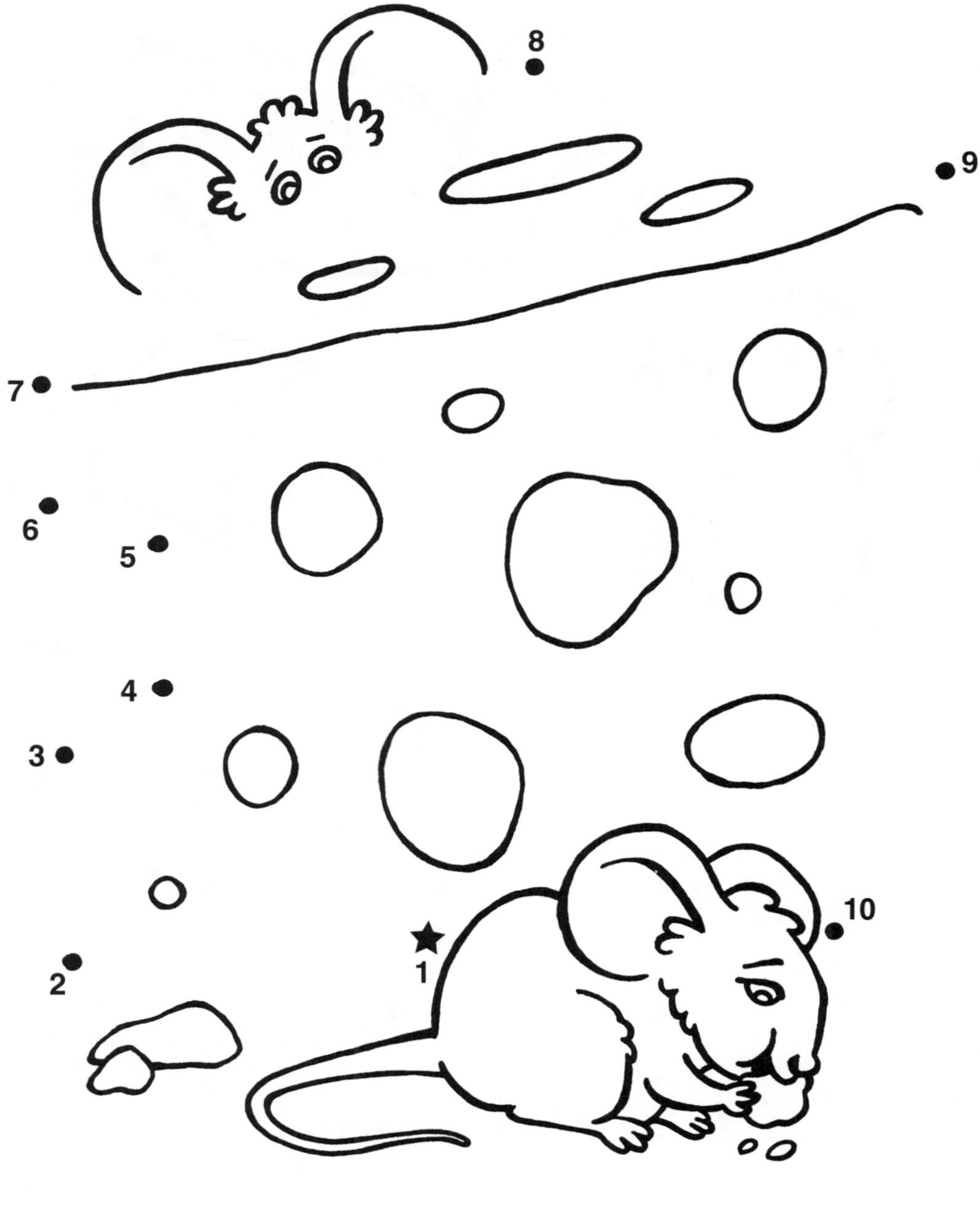

# Paintbrush (1-11)

# Spider Web (1-12)

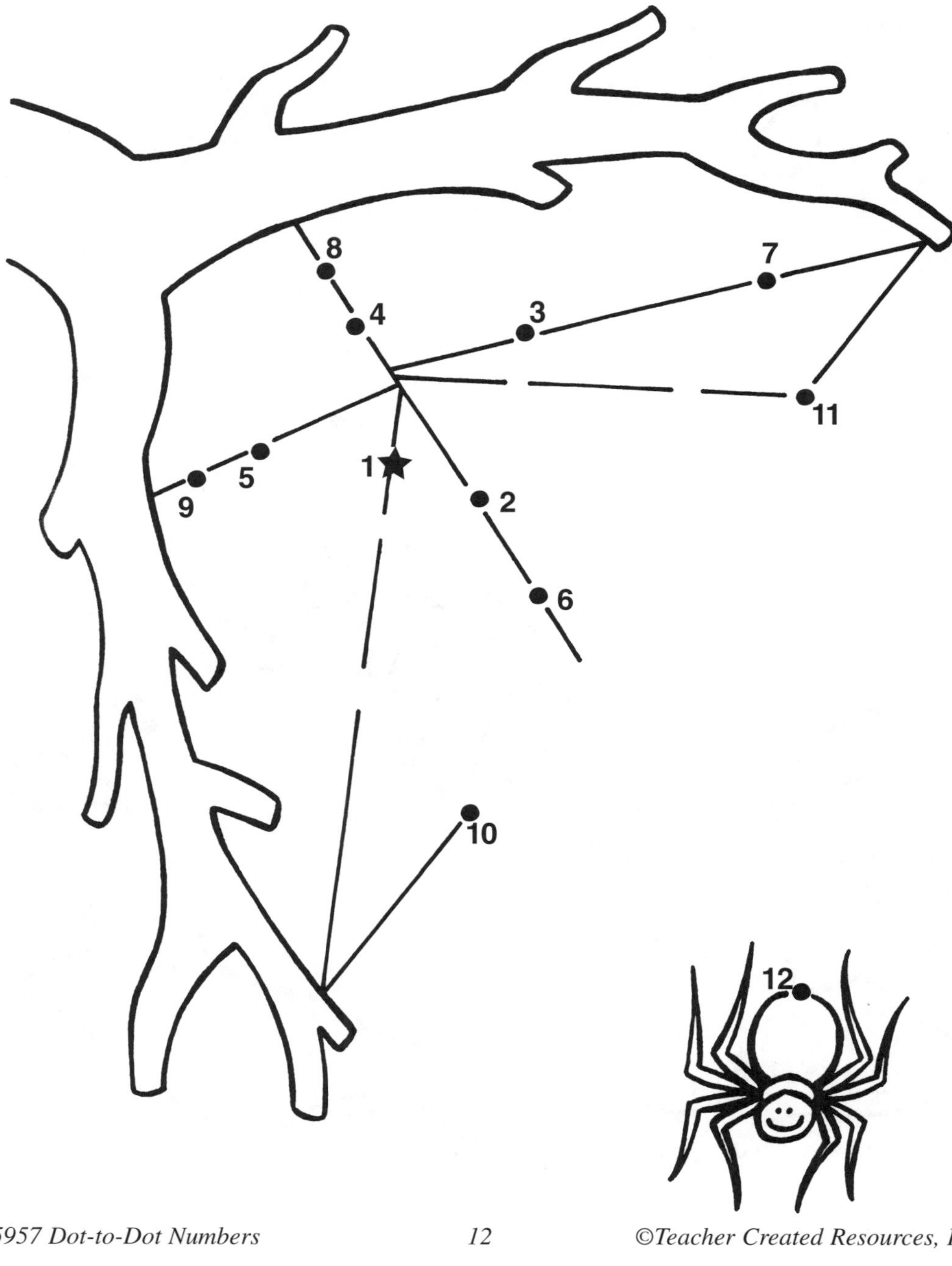


 

# Drink It Up! (1-13)

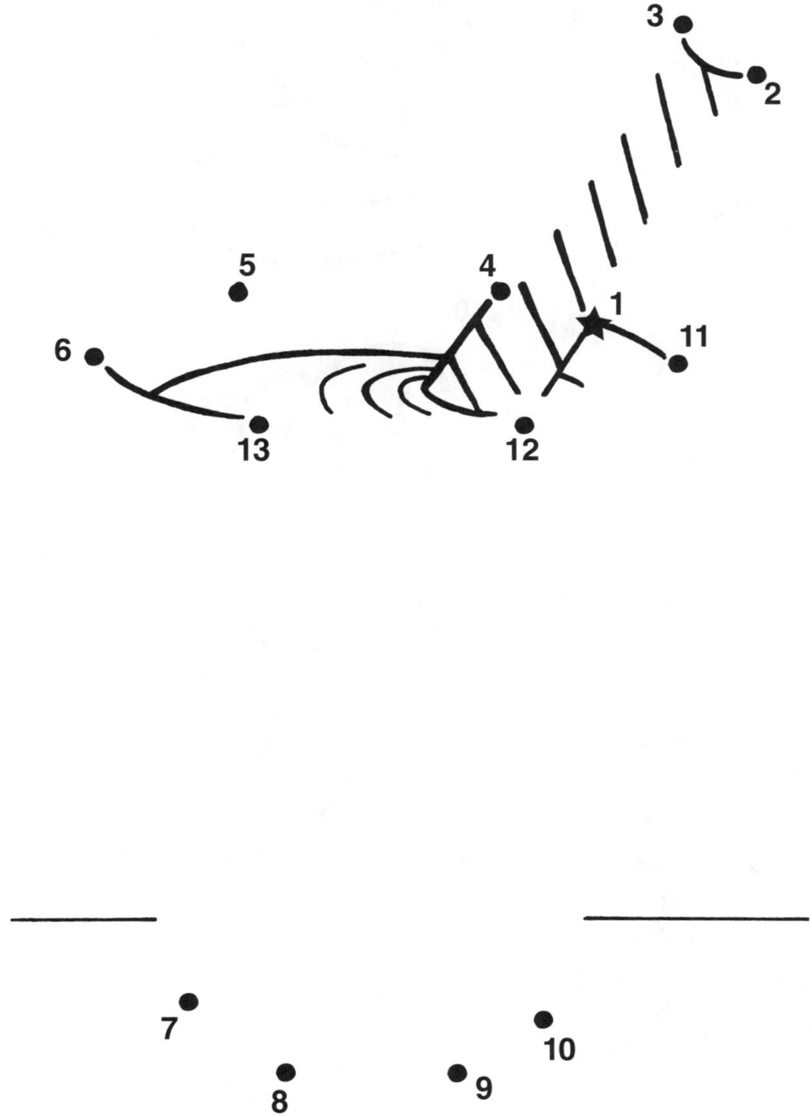

# Fish (1-13)

# Toss the Ball (1-14)

# Bring Me Luck (1-15)

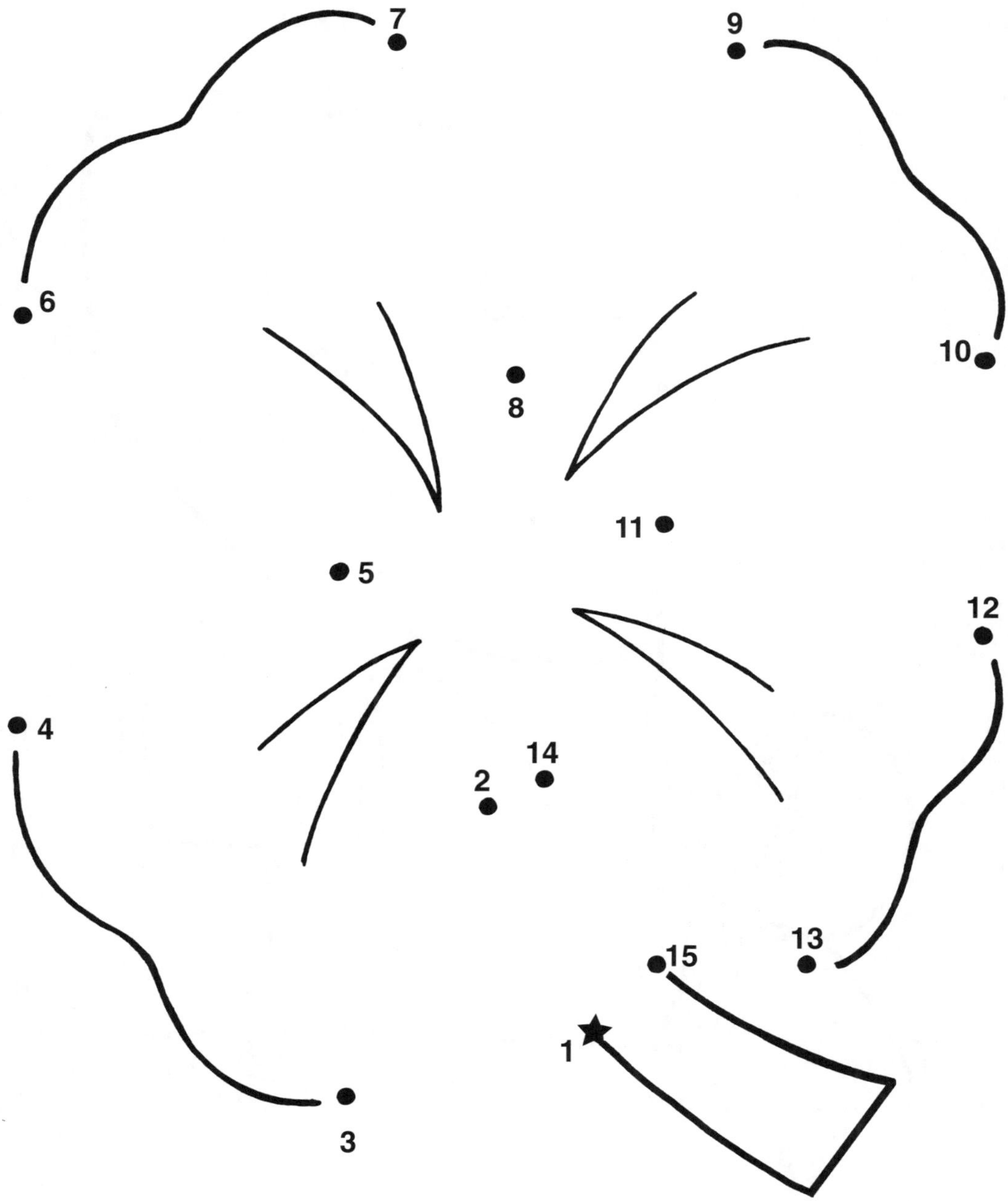

# Brrr! (1-15)

# Home Run (1-15)

# Valentine (1-15)

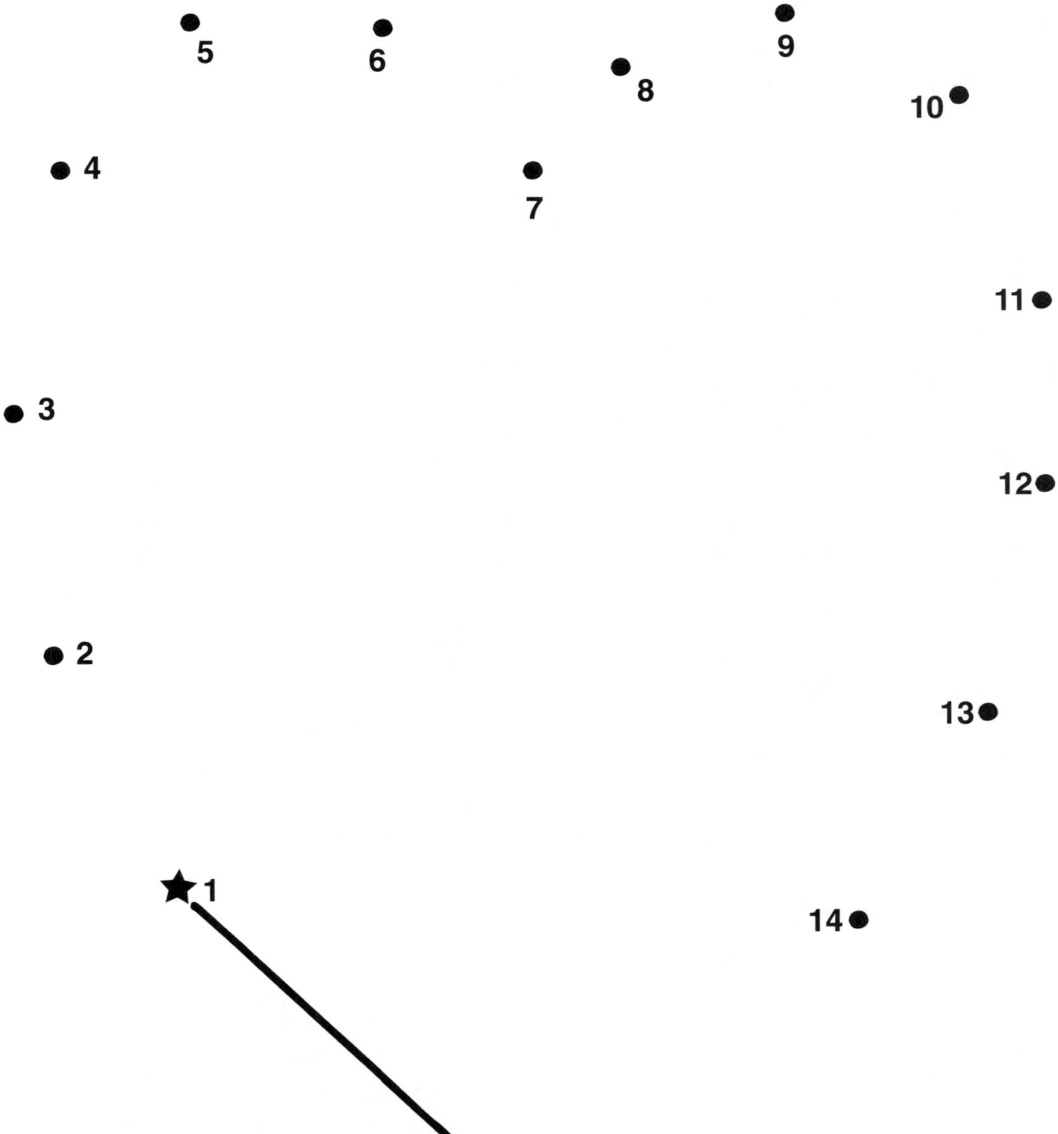

# Harvest Time (1-15)

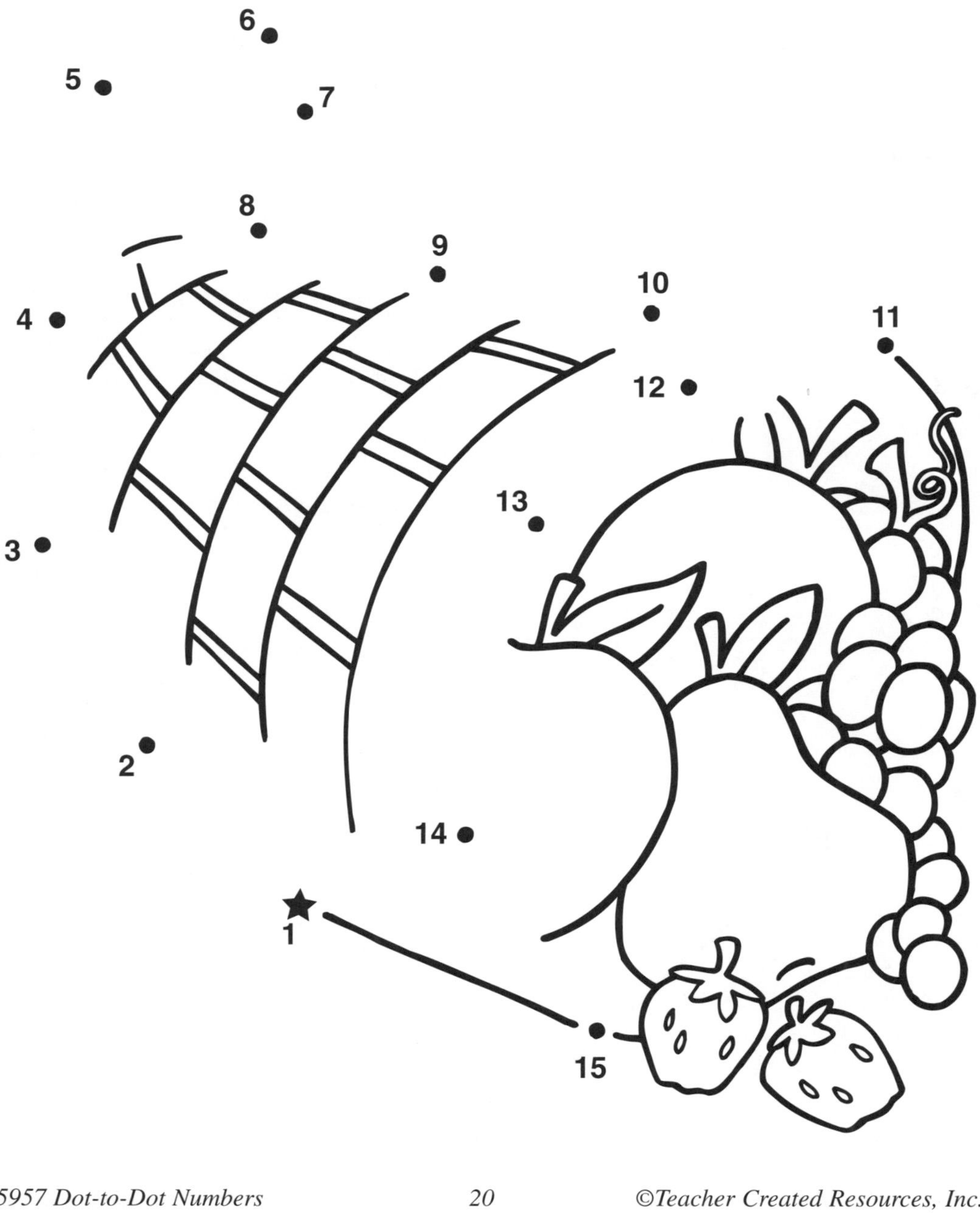

# The Winner Is . . . (1-15)

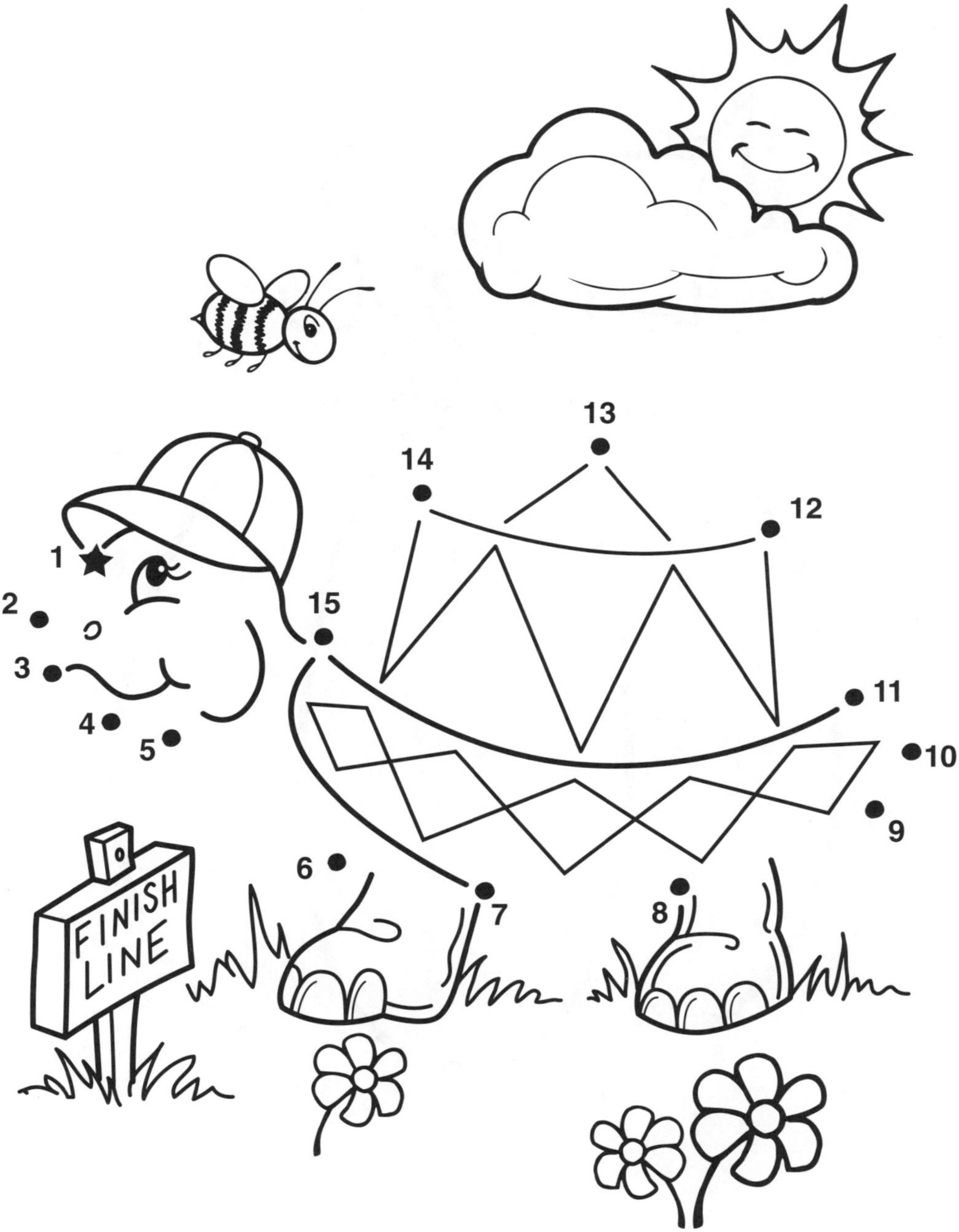

# In the Garden (1-15)

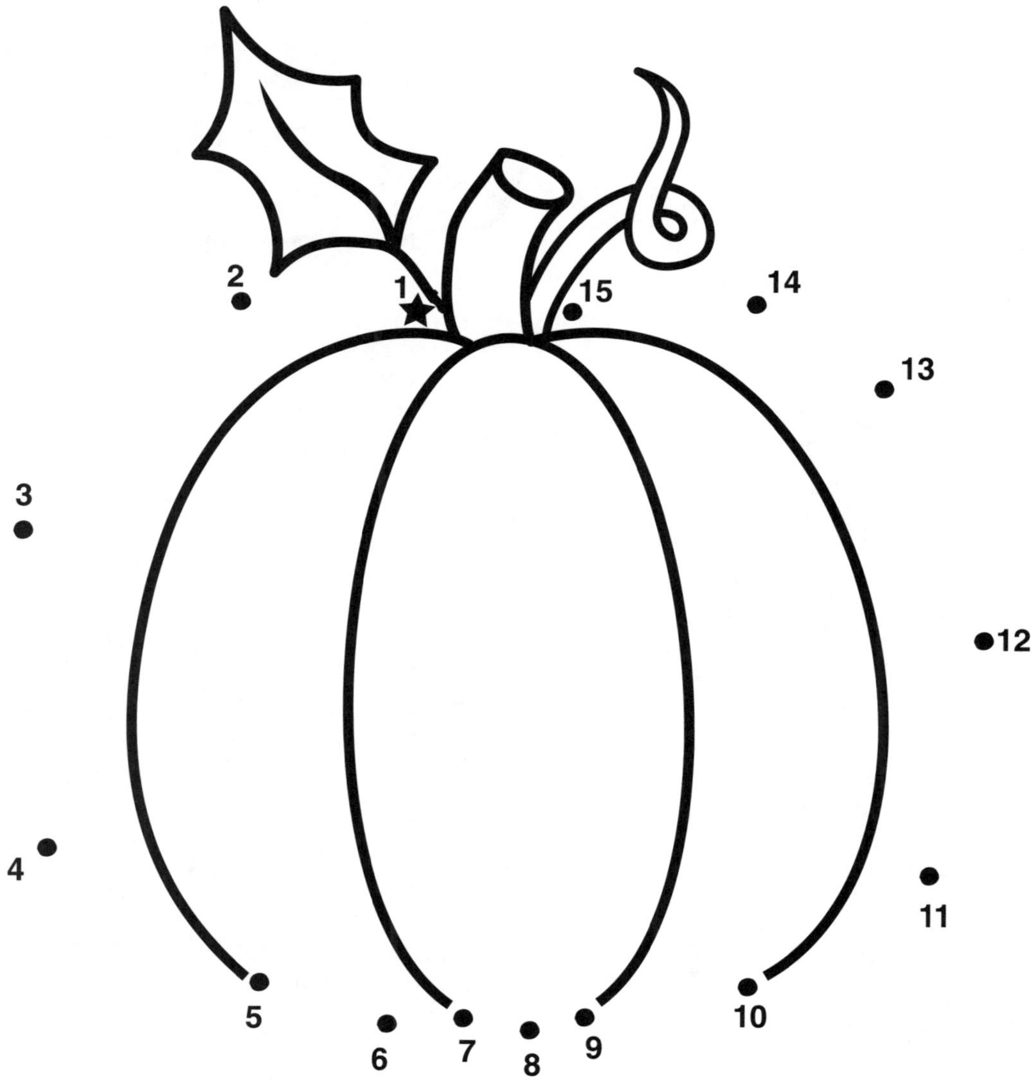

# Surf the Wave (1-15)

# Float Down (1-16)

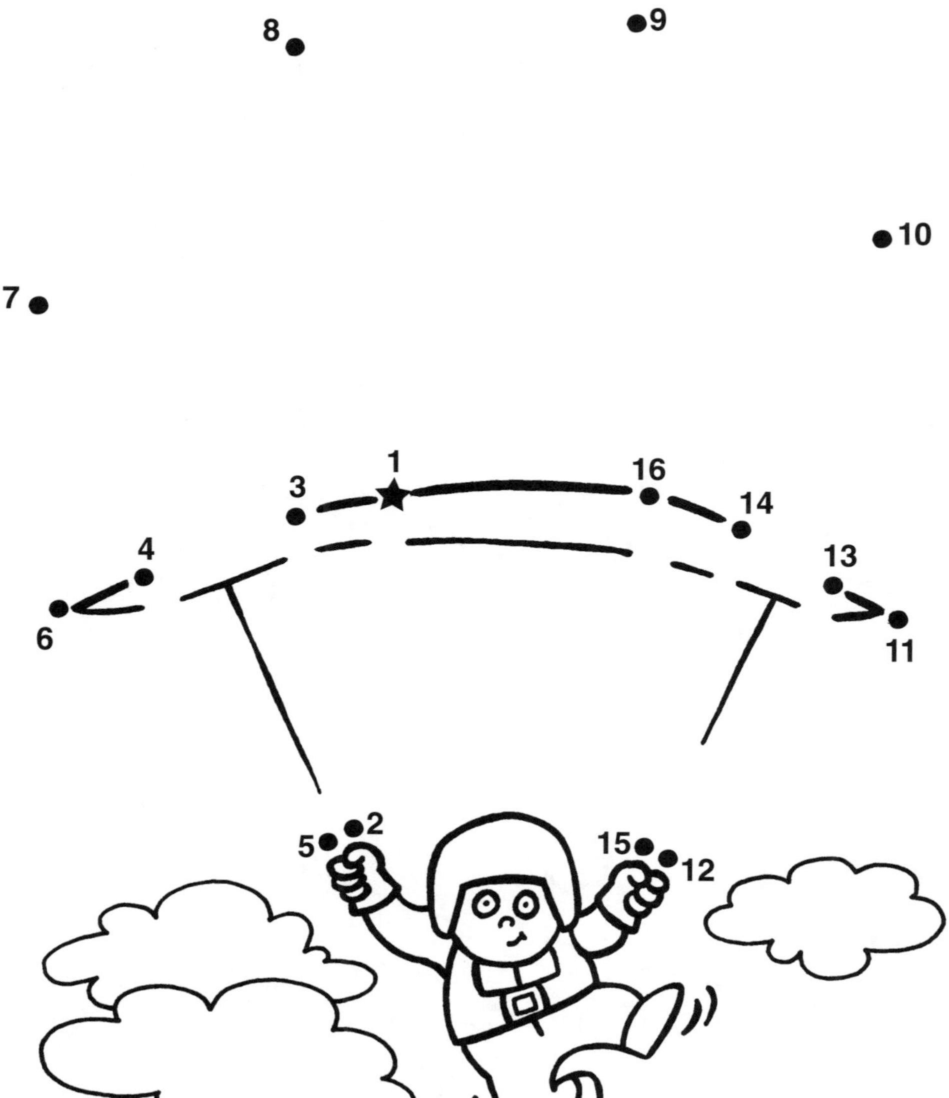

# Where's the Bone?
(1-17)

# Candlelight (1-18)

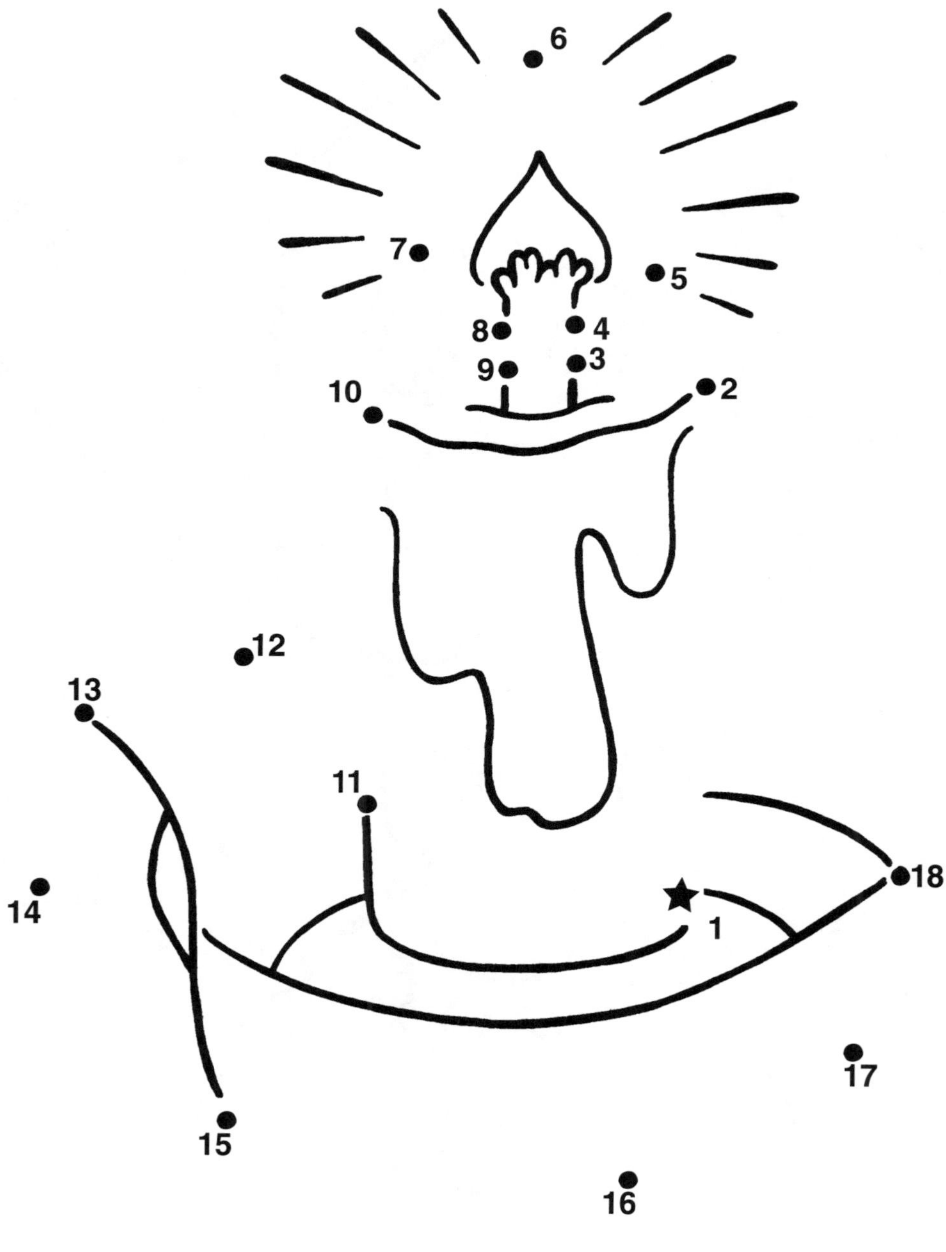

# Help Fight Fire (1-18)

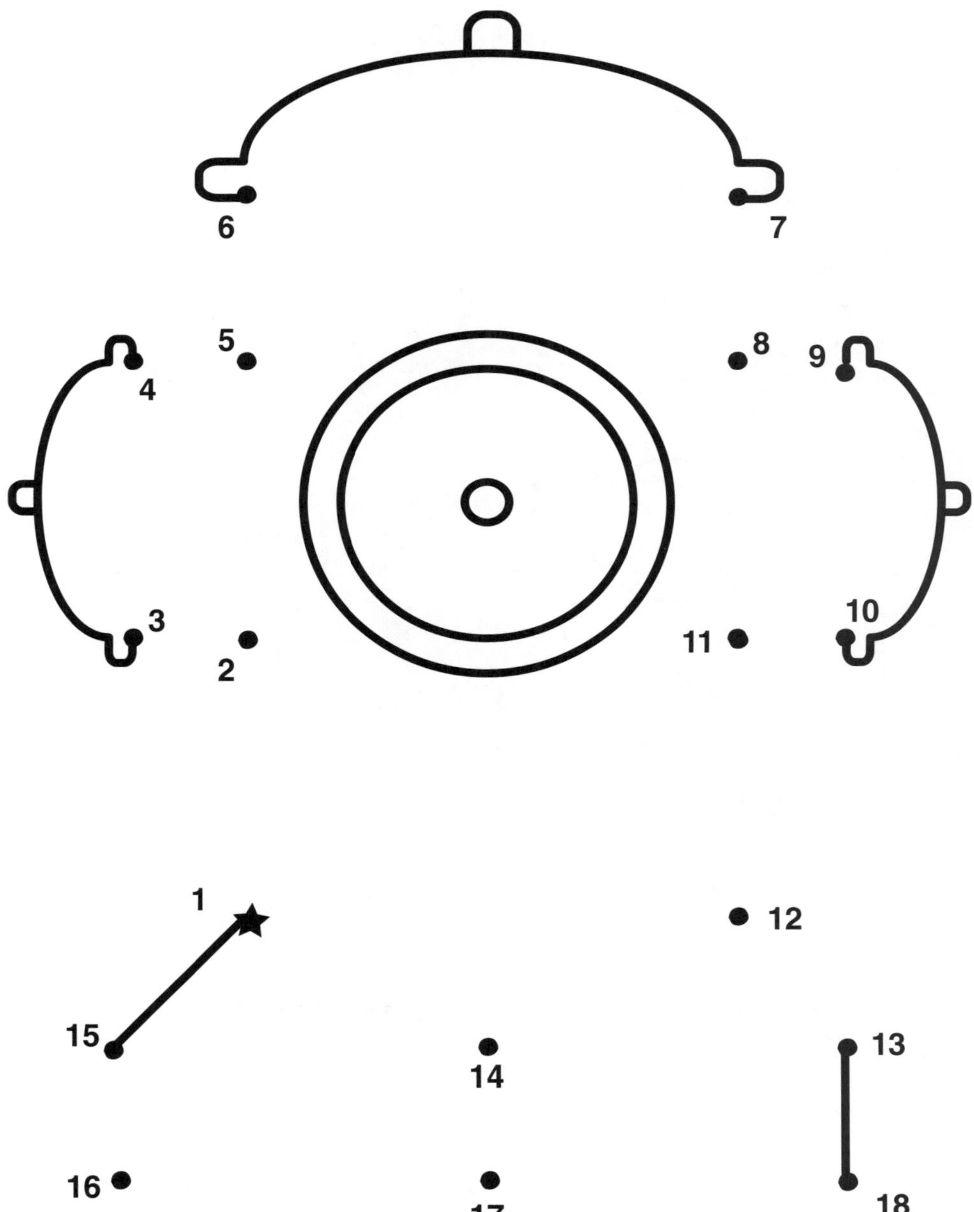

# Fishbowl (1-18)

# An Apple a Day (1-19)

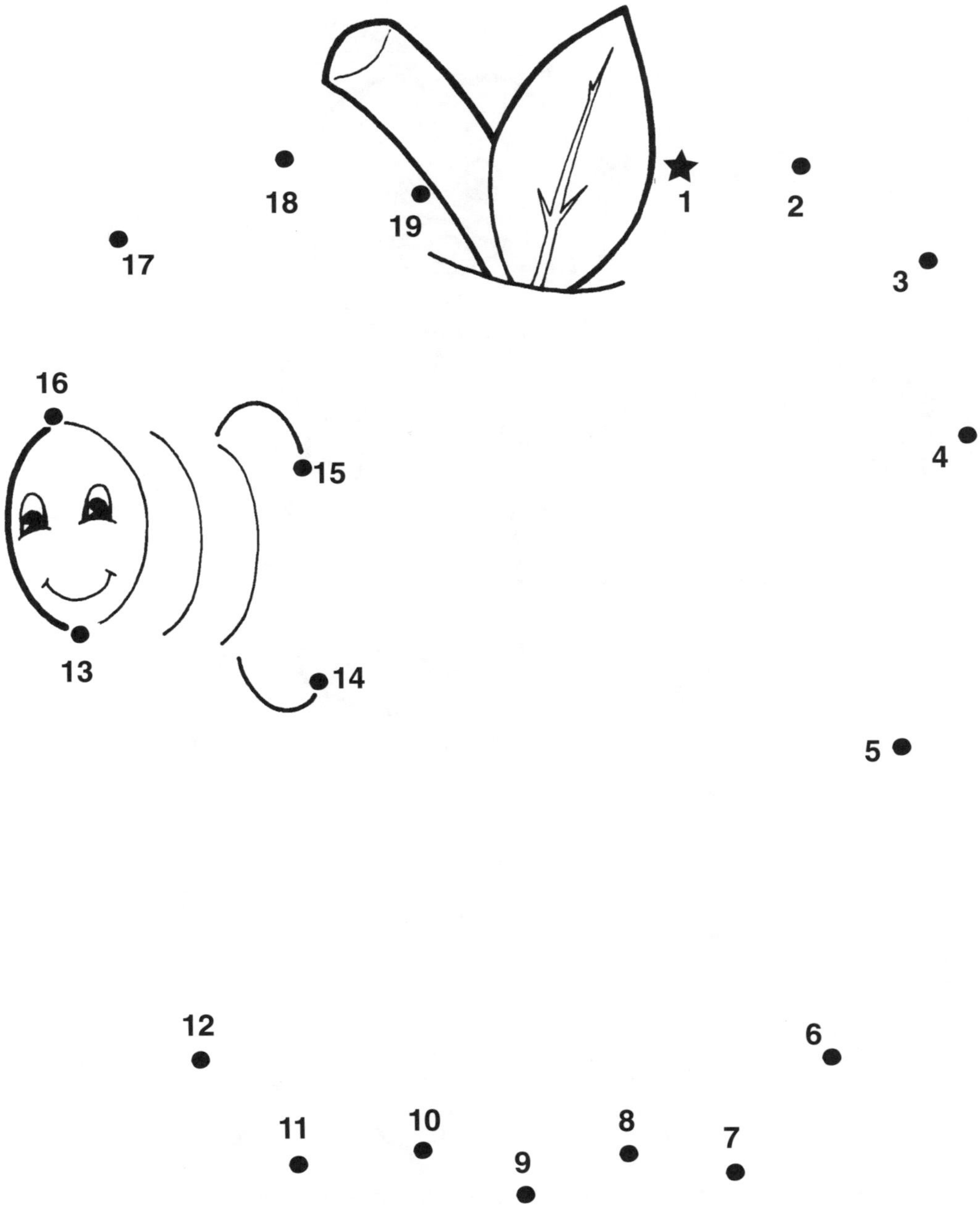

# Dancing Penguin (1-20)

# Where's the Bunny Hiding? (1-20)

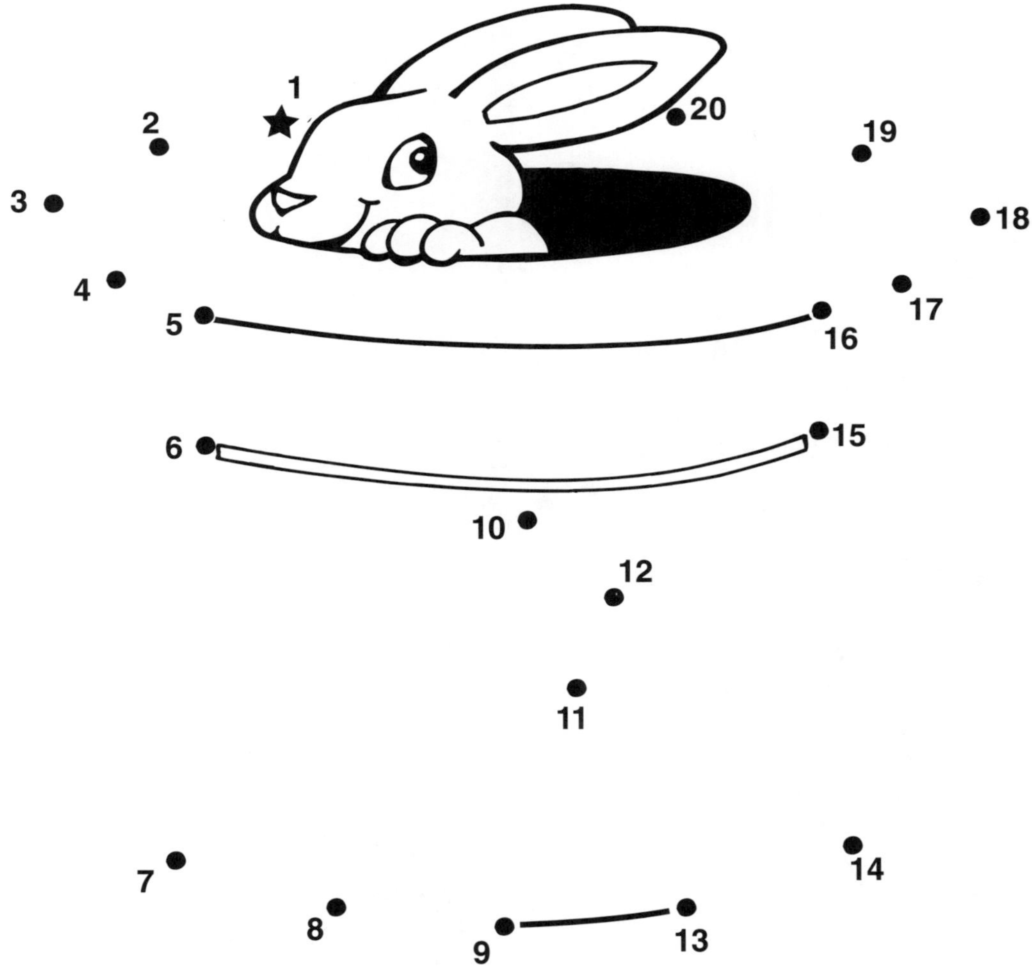

# Celebrate! (1-20)

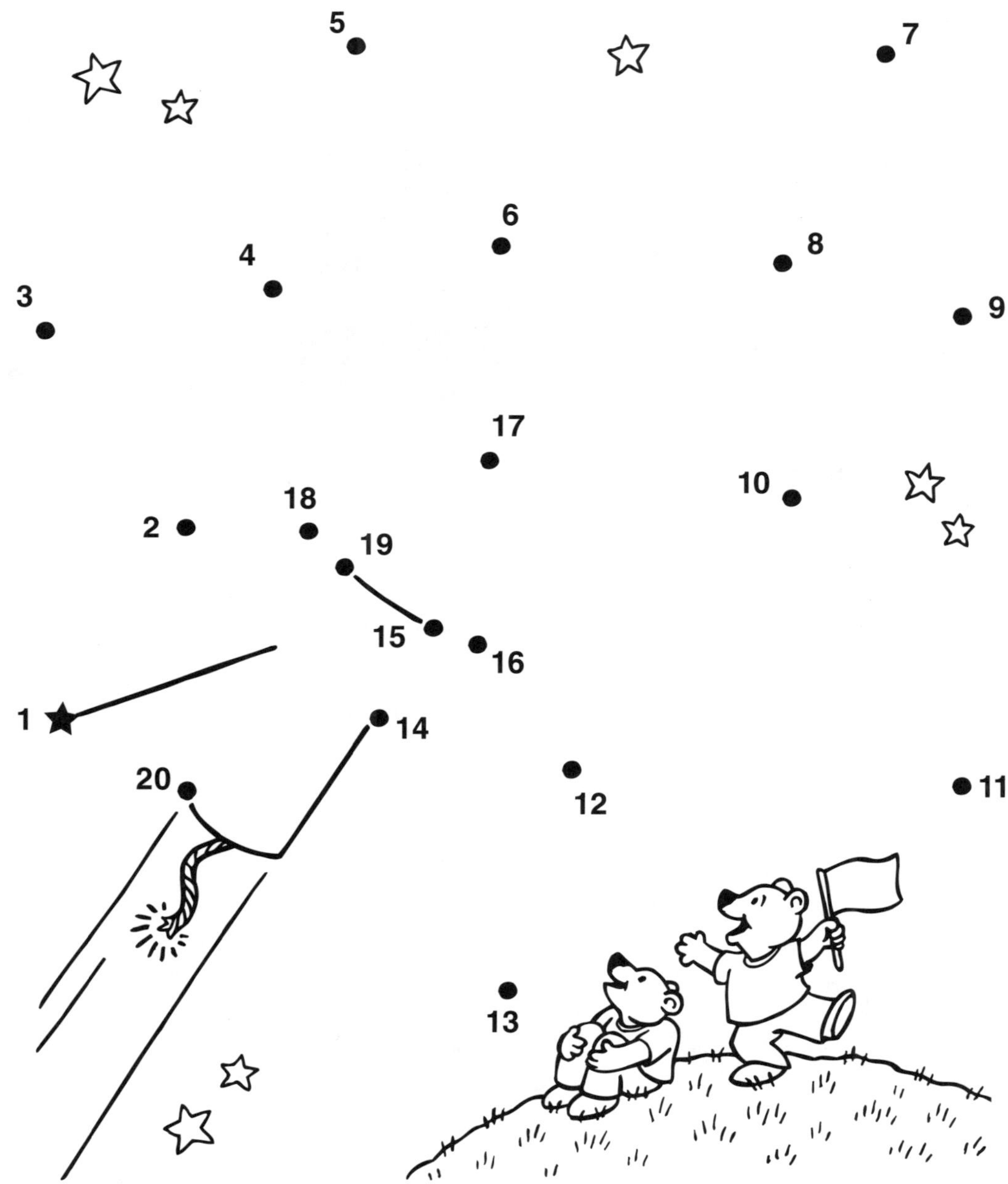

# High Flying (1-20)

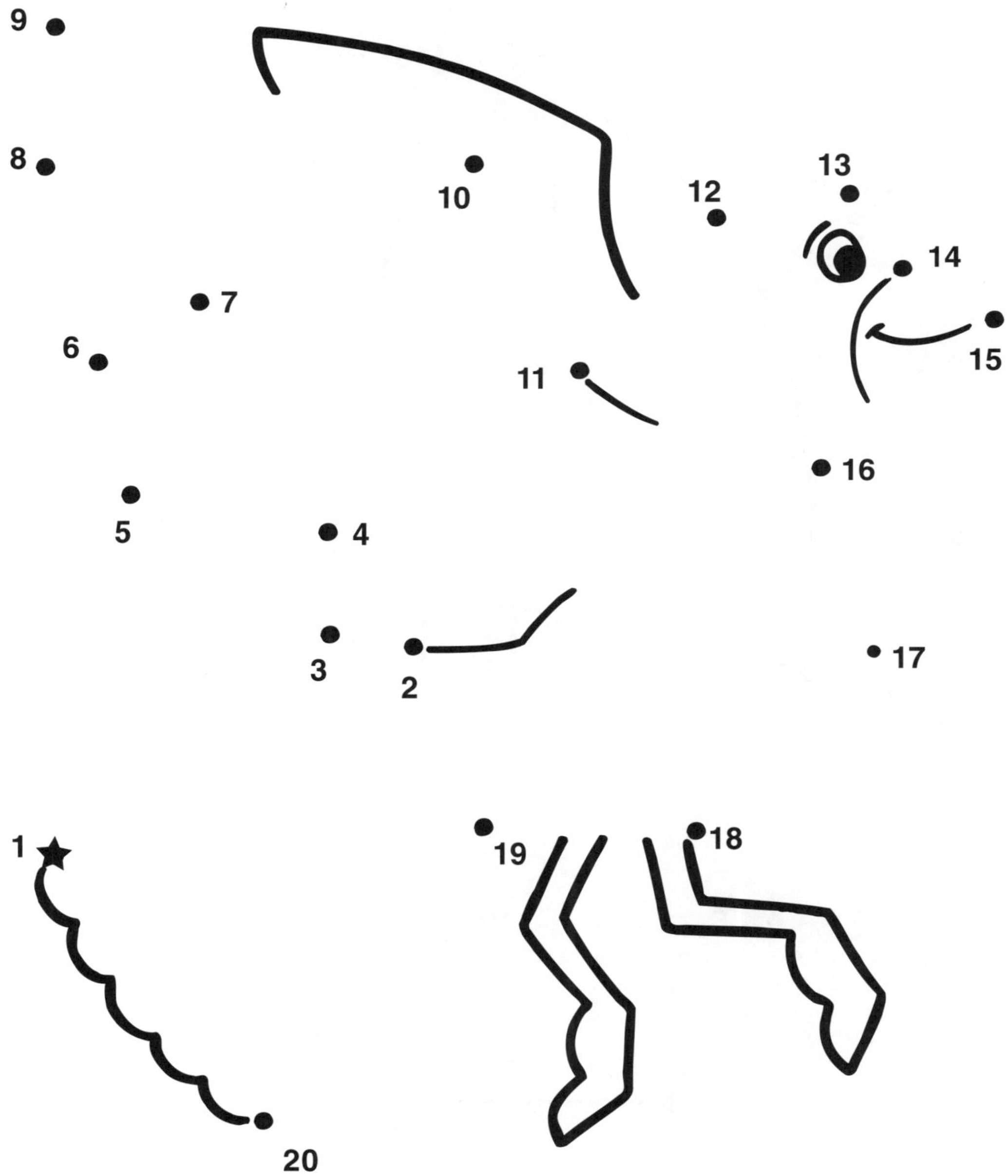

# It Is Raining (1-20)

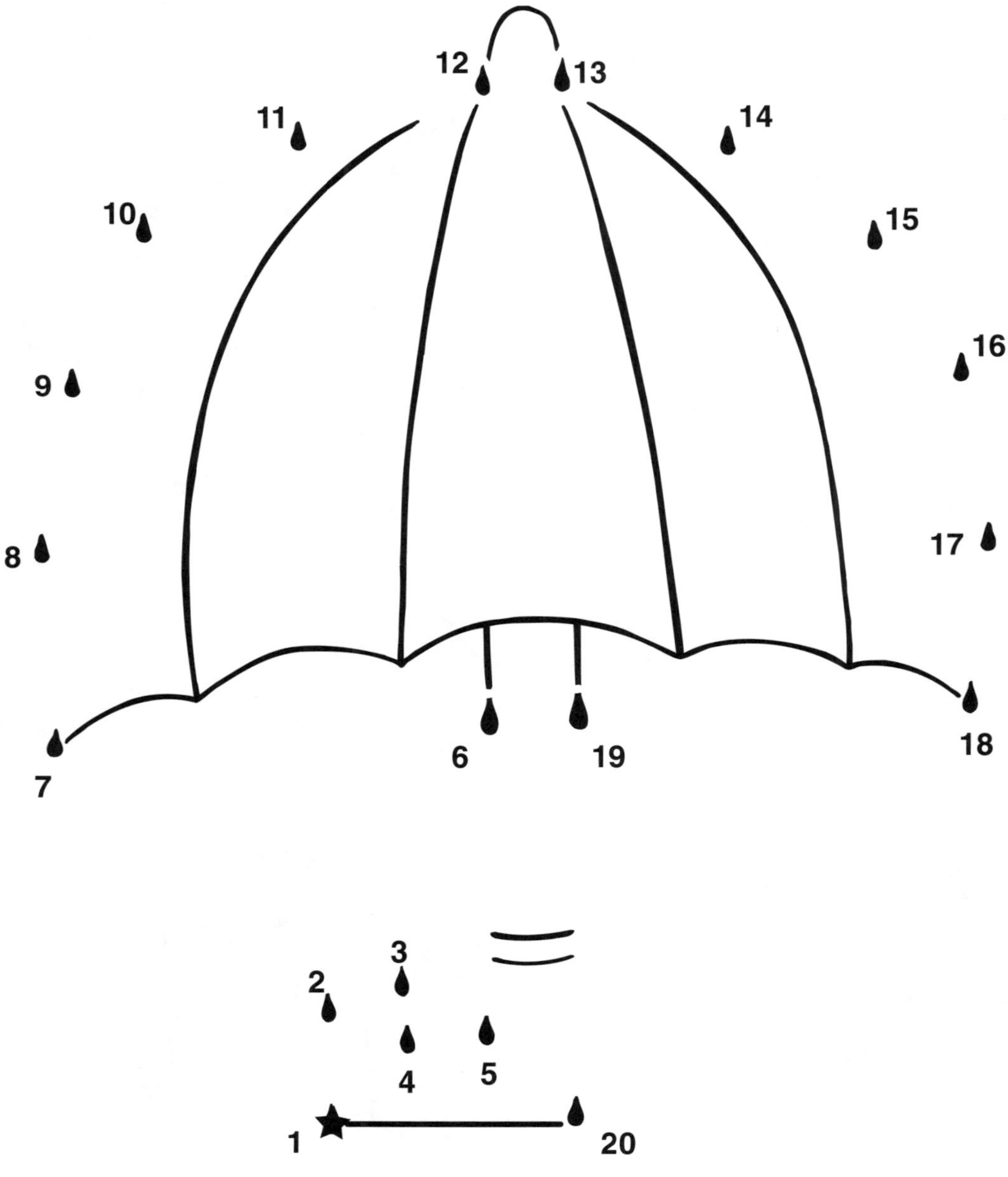

# Bird in a Cage (1-20)

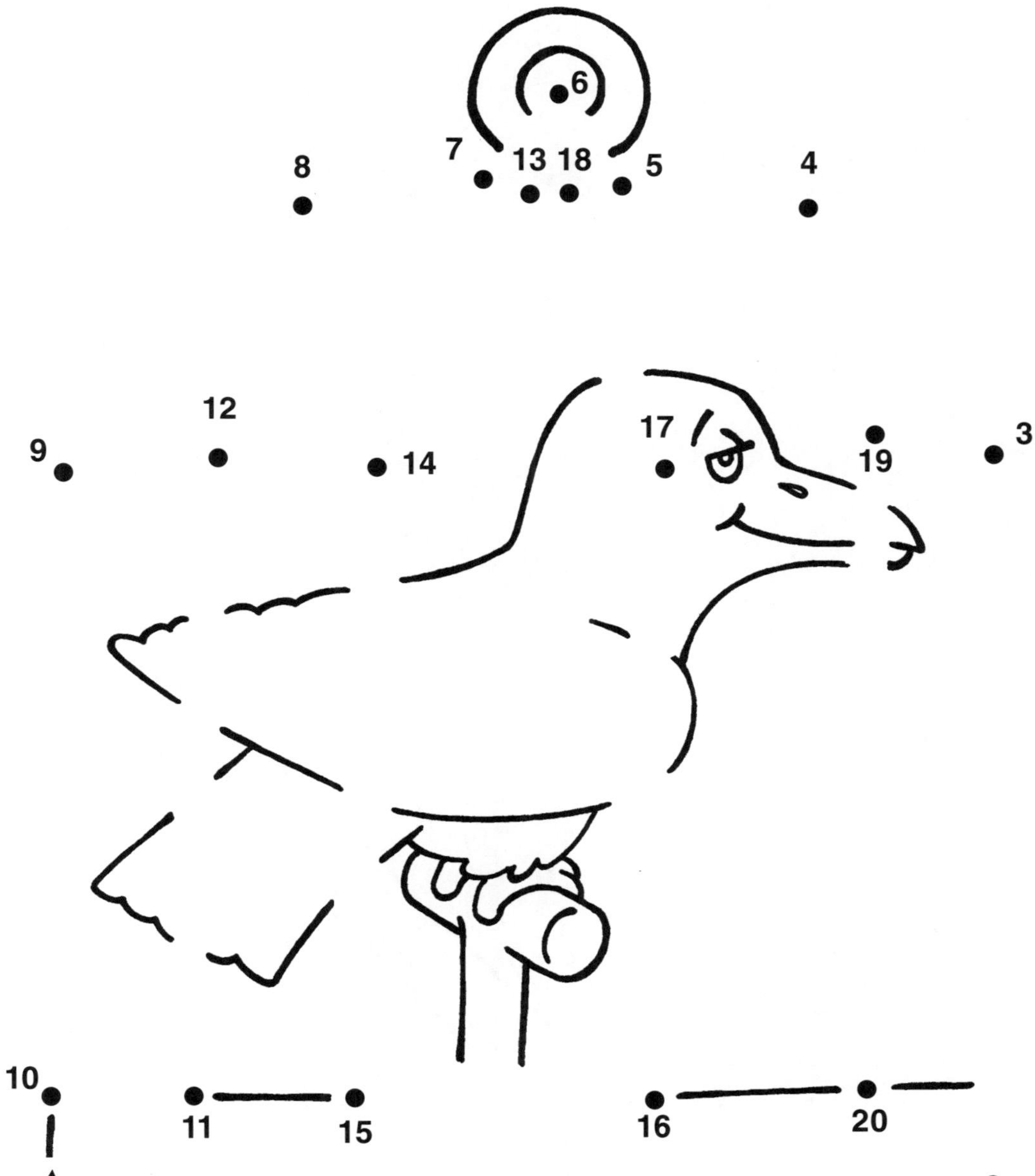

# Dental Care (1-20)

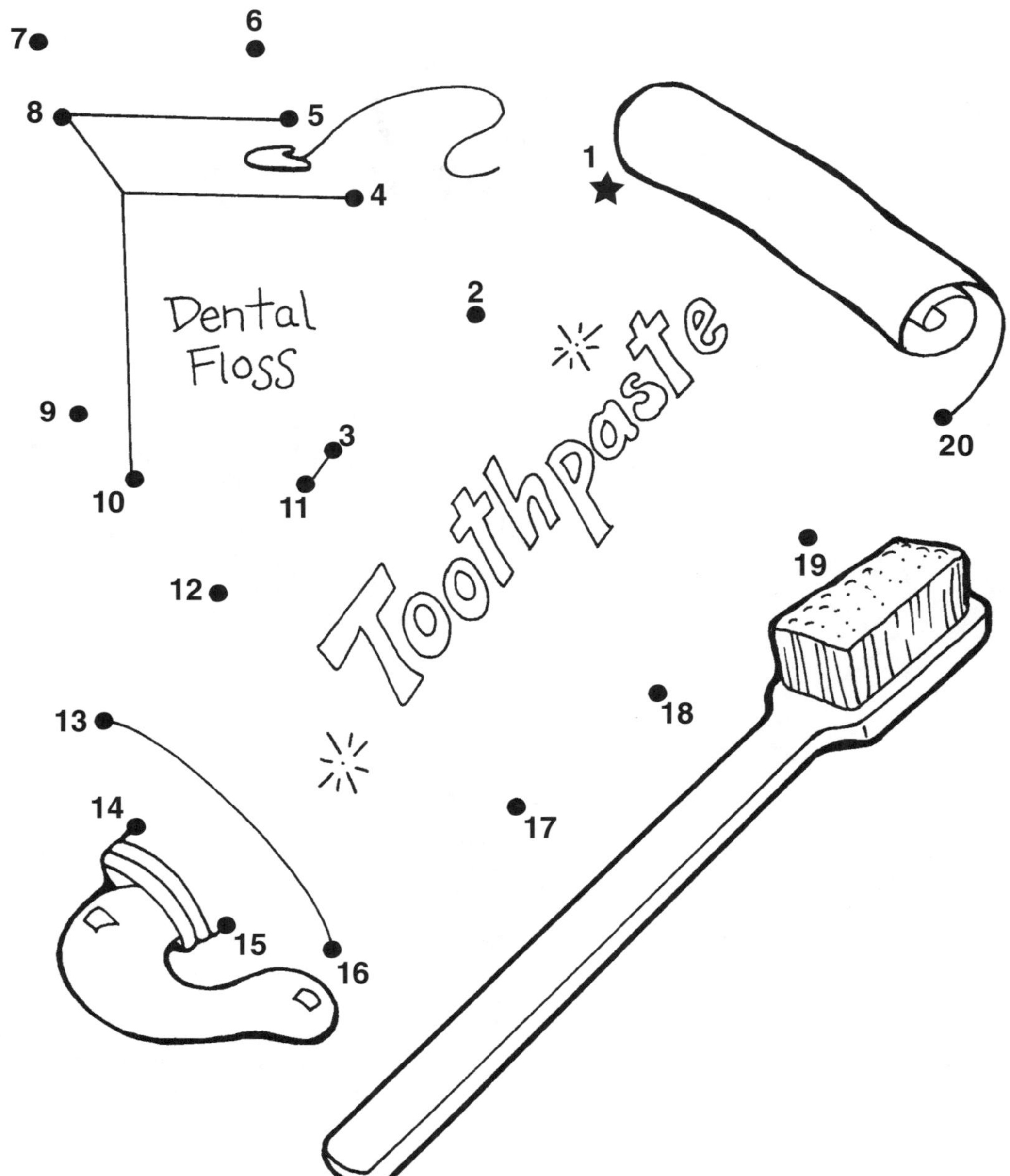

# Where Do the Animals Live? (1-20)

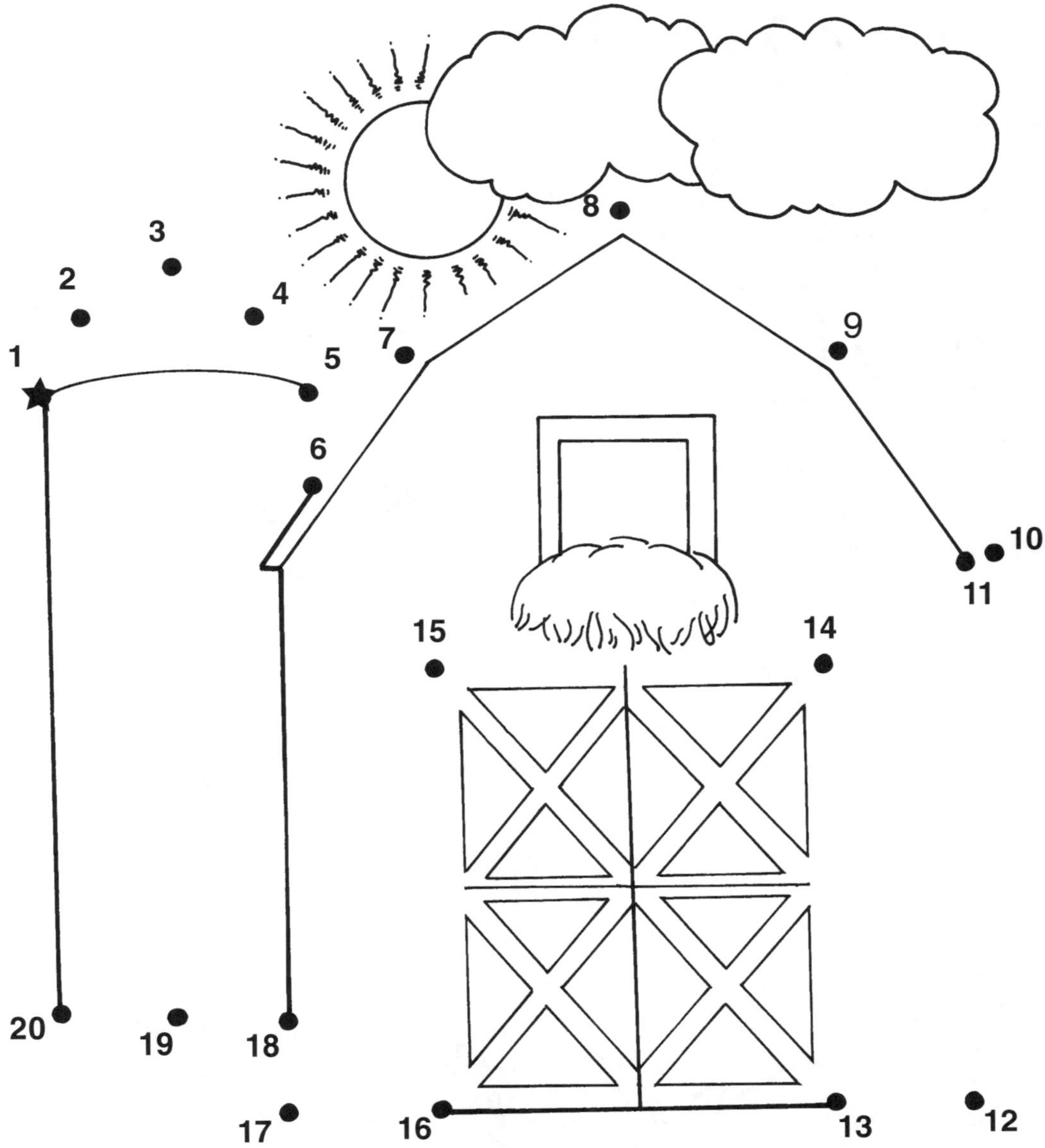

# Splash! (1-20)

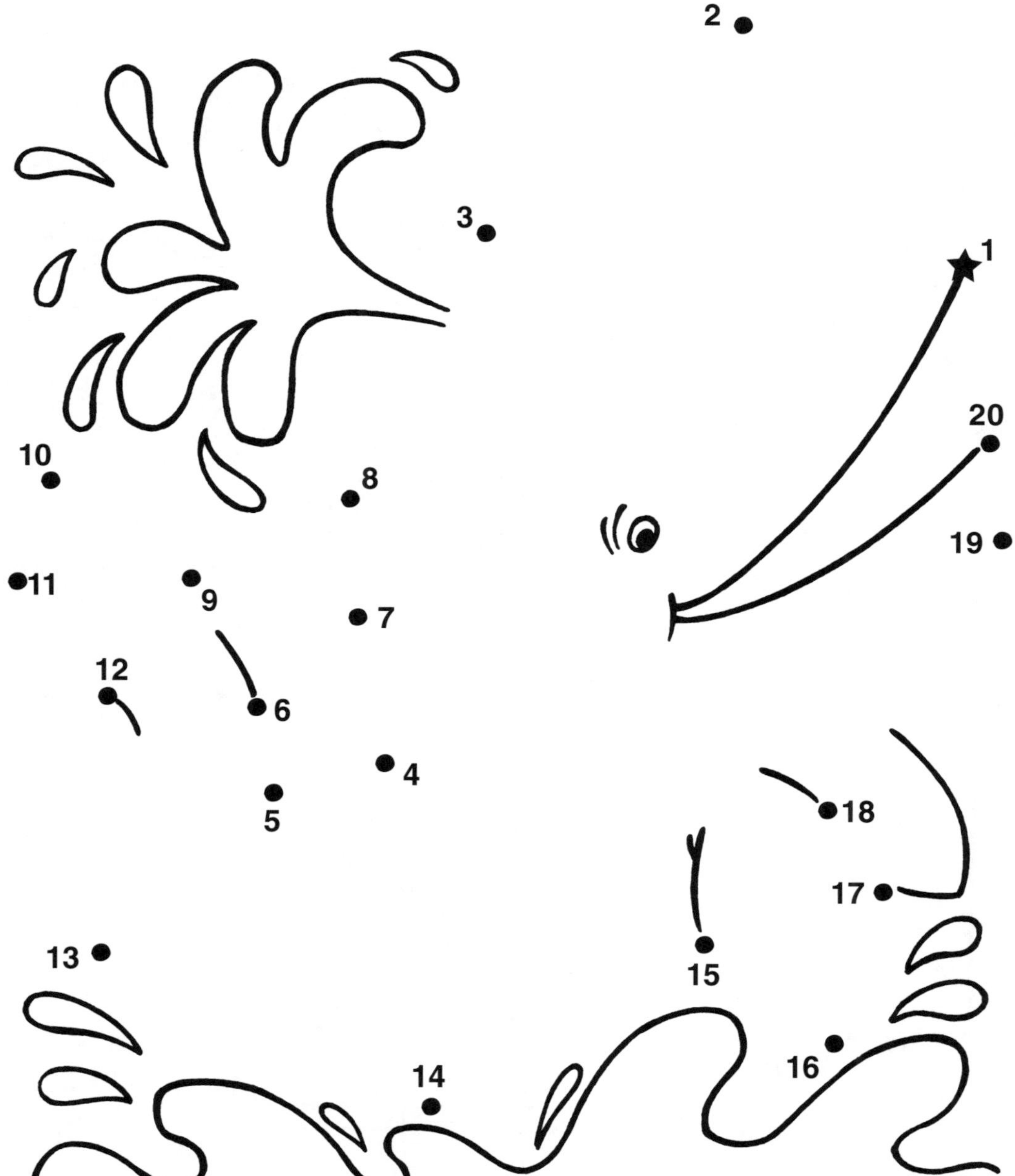

# Time to Nest (1-21)

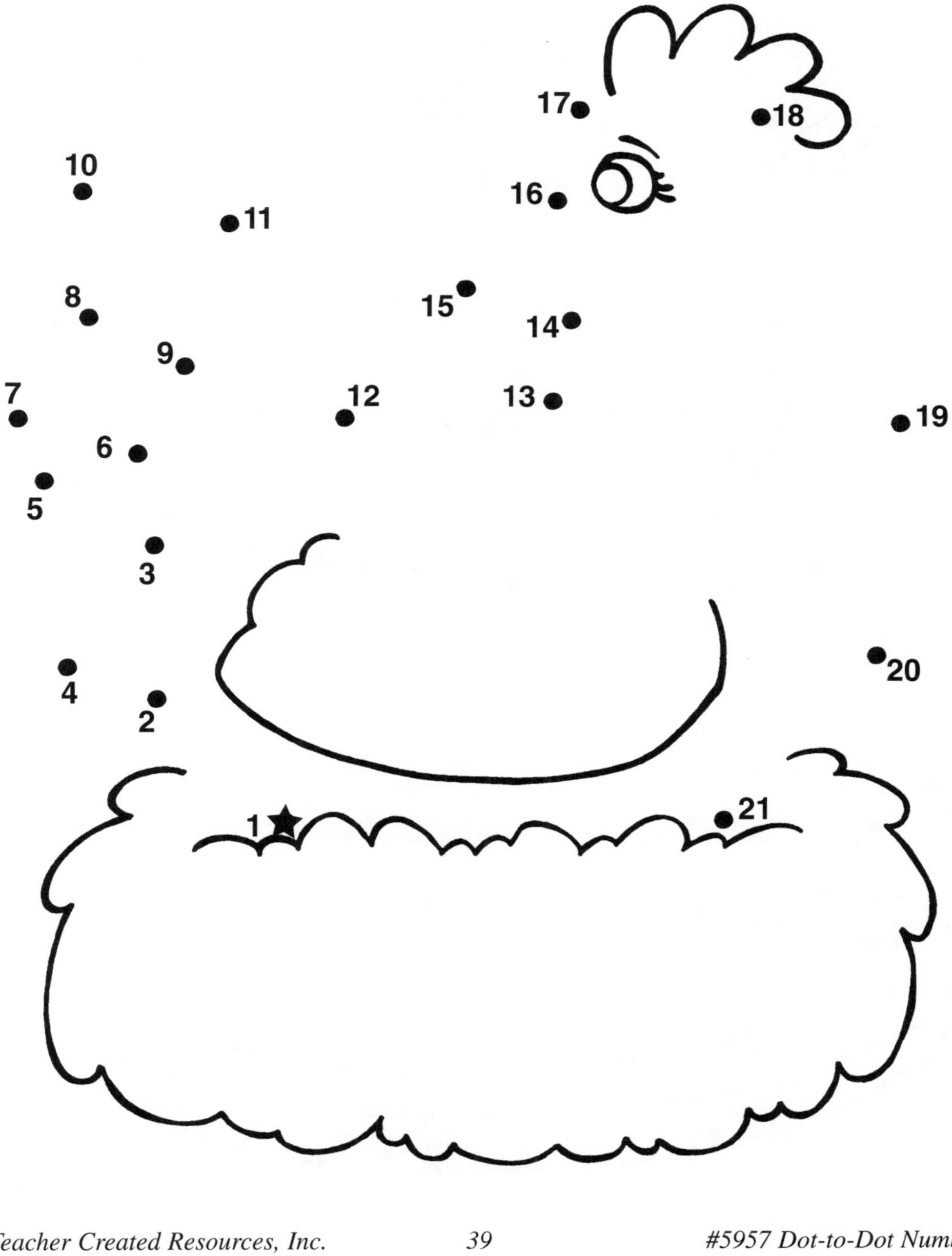

# Happy Birthday (1-22)

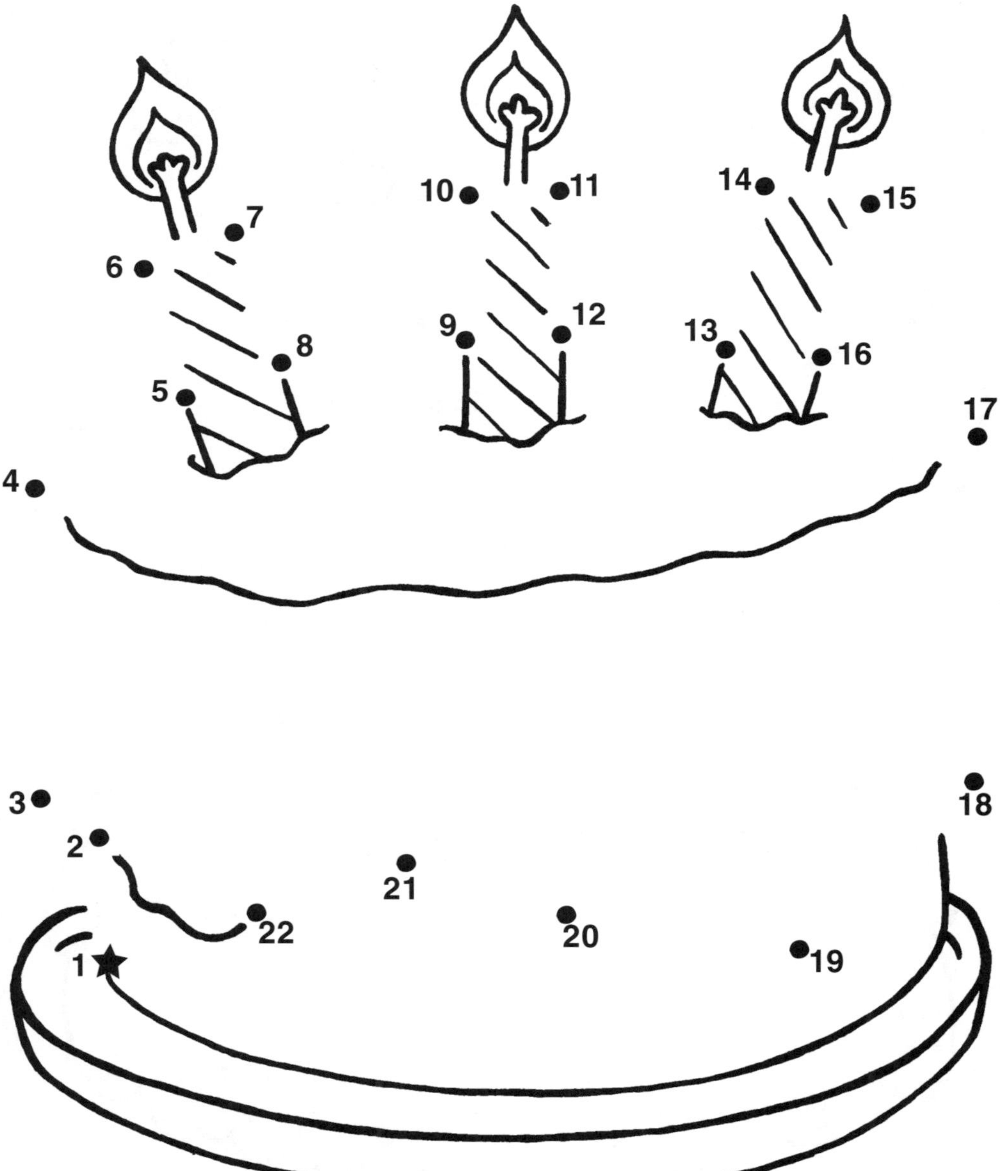

# Shoe (1-22)

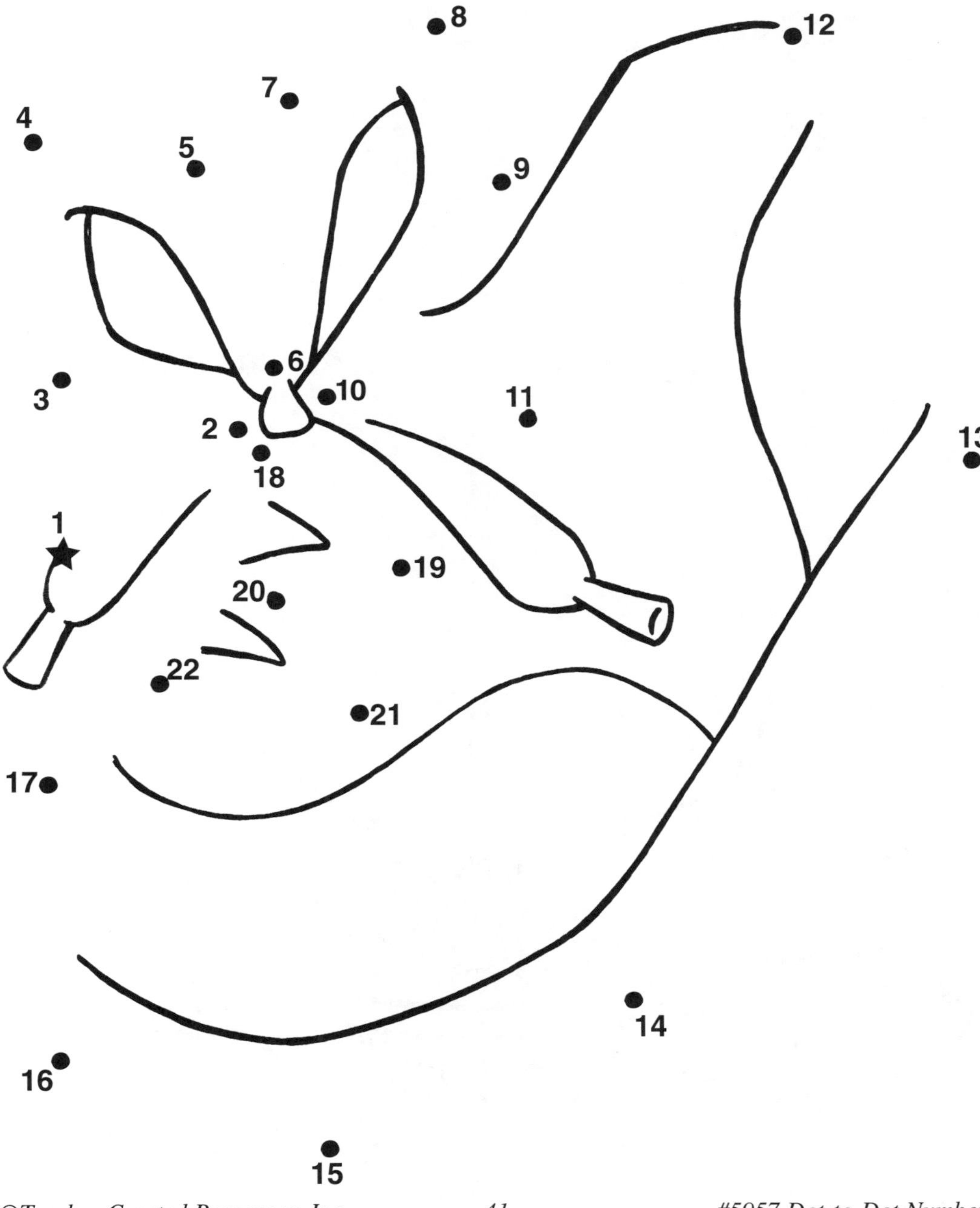

# Hot Air Balloon (1-23)

# Snail (1-24)

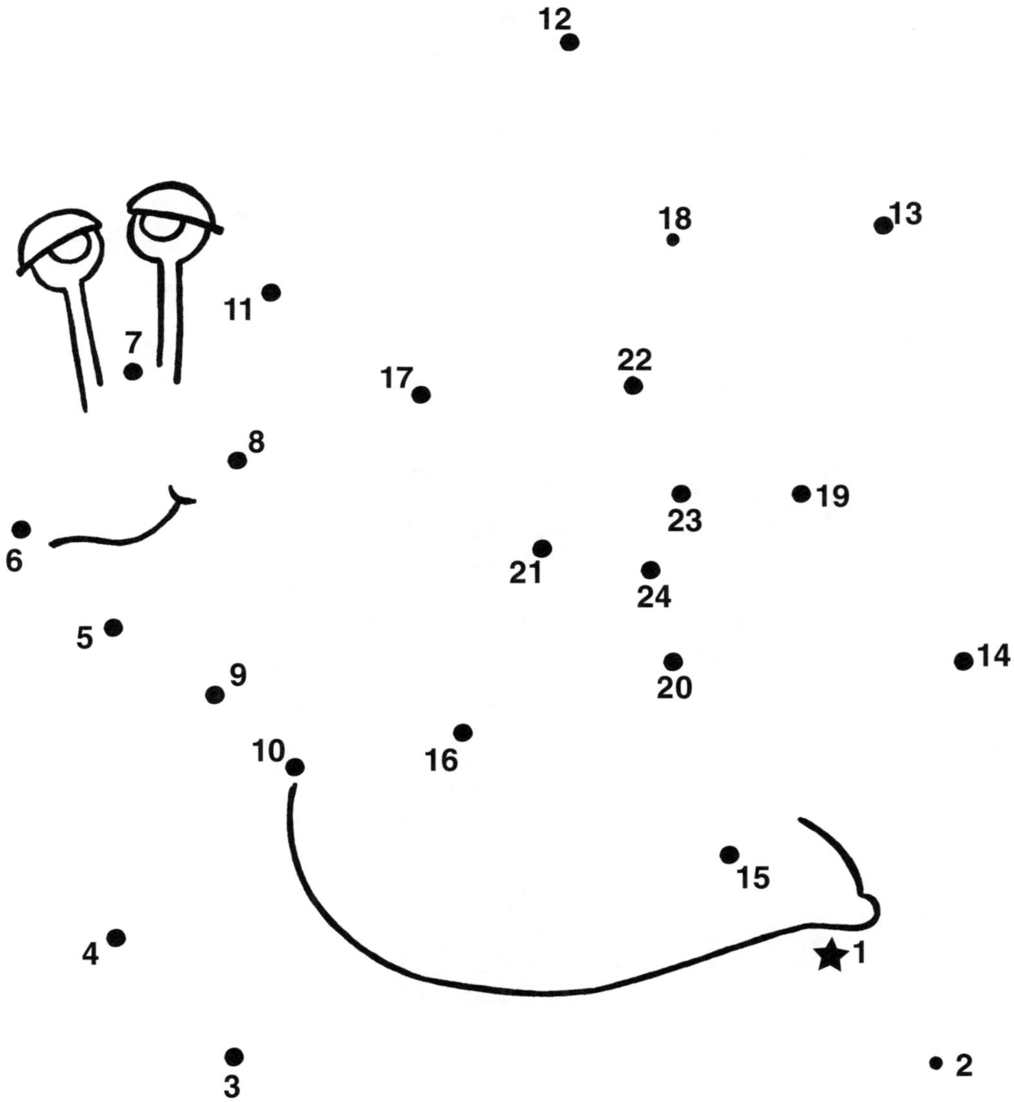

# Gumball Goodies (1-25)

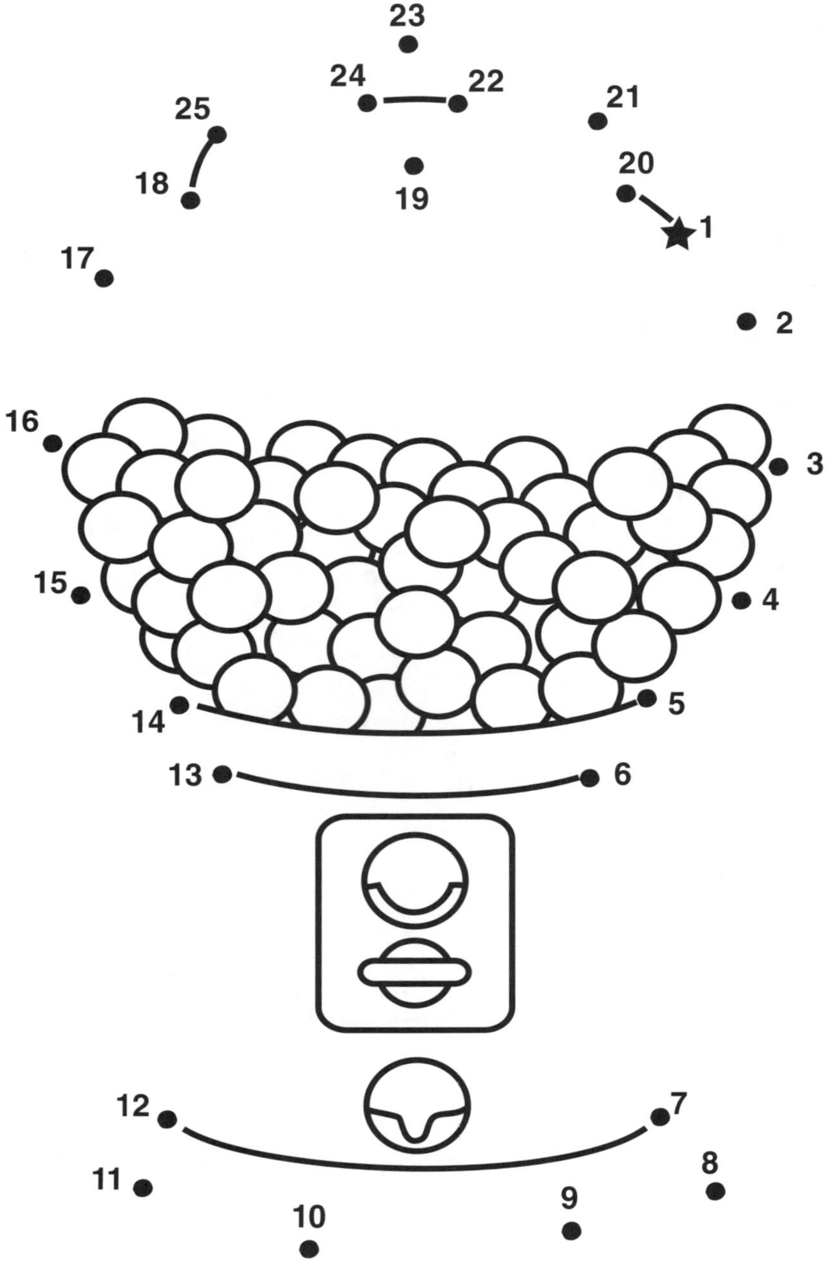

# Heading Home (1-25)

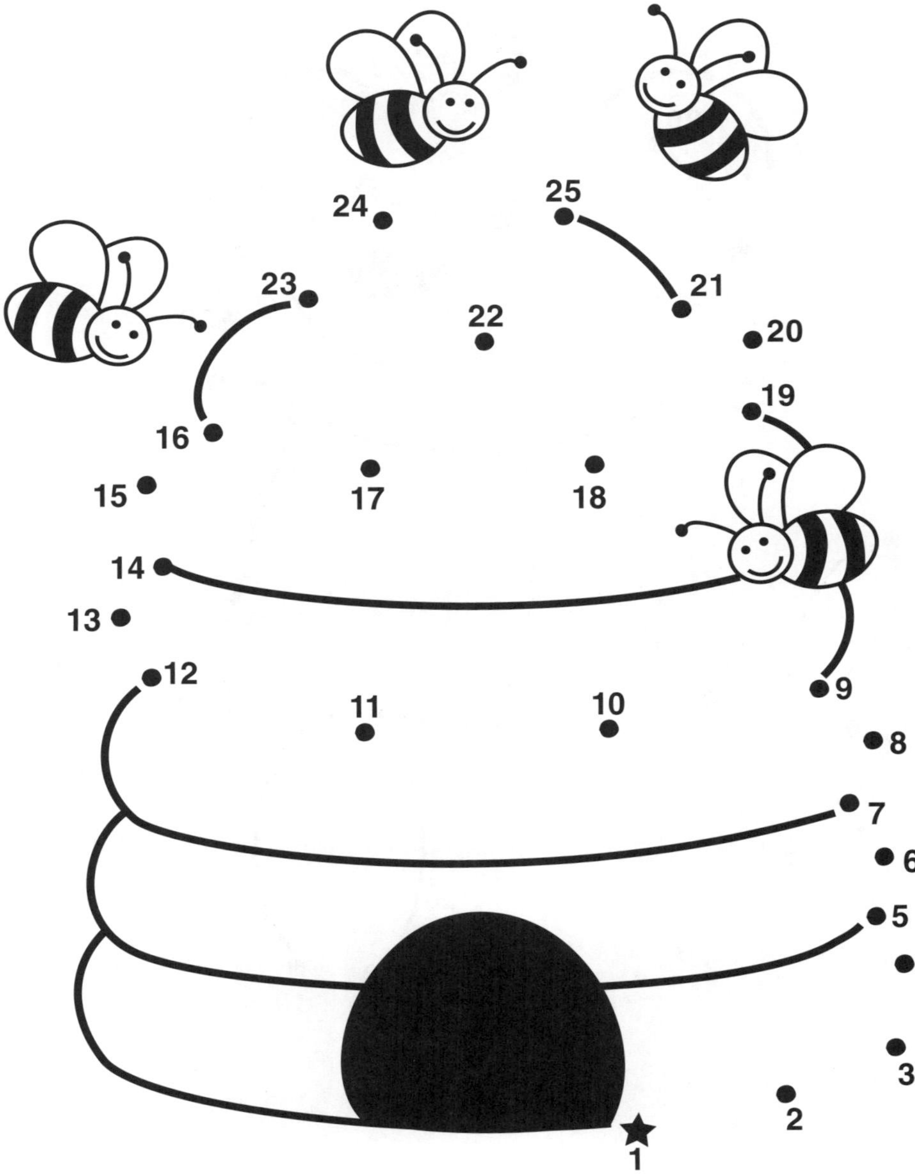

# Cuddle Buddy (1-25)

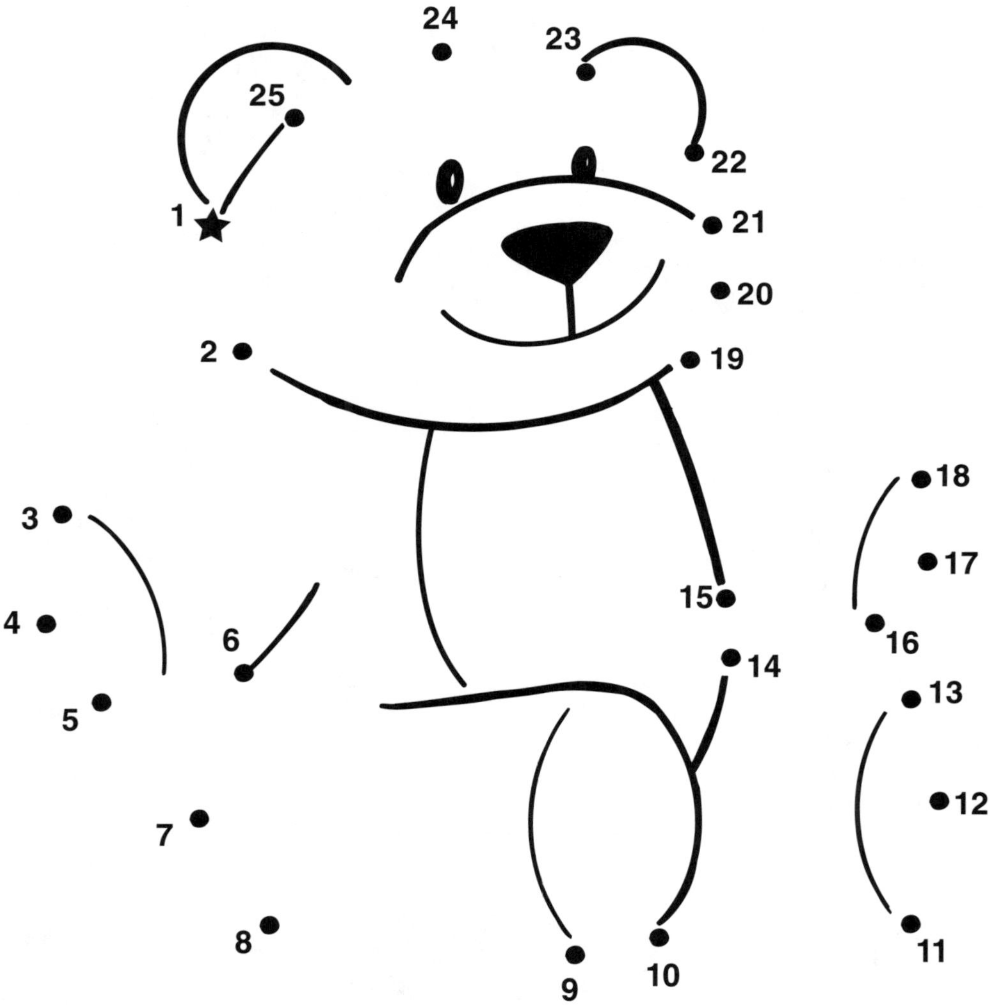


 

# A Special Treat (1-25)

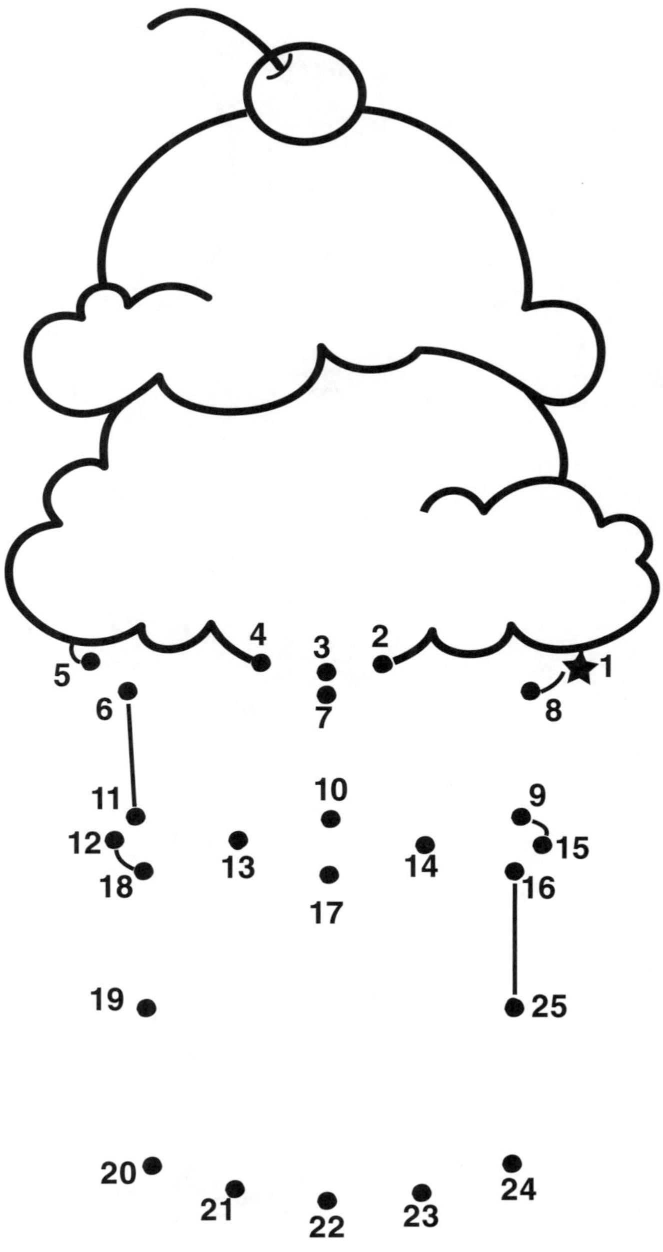

# Sea Lion (1-25)

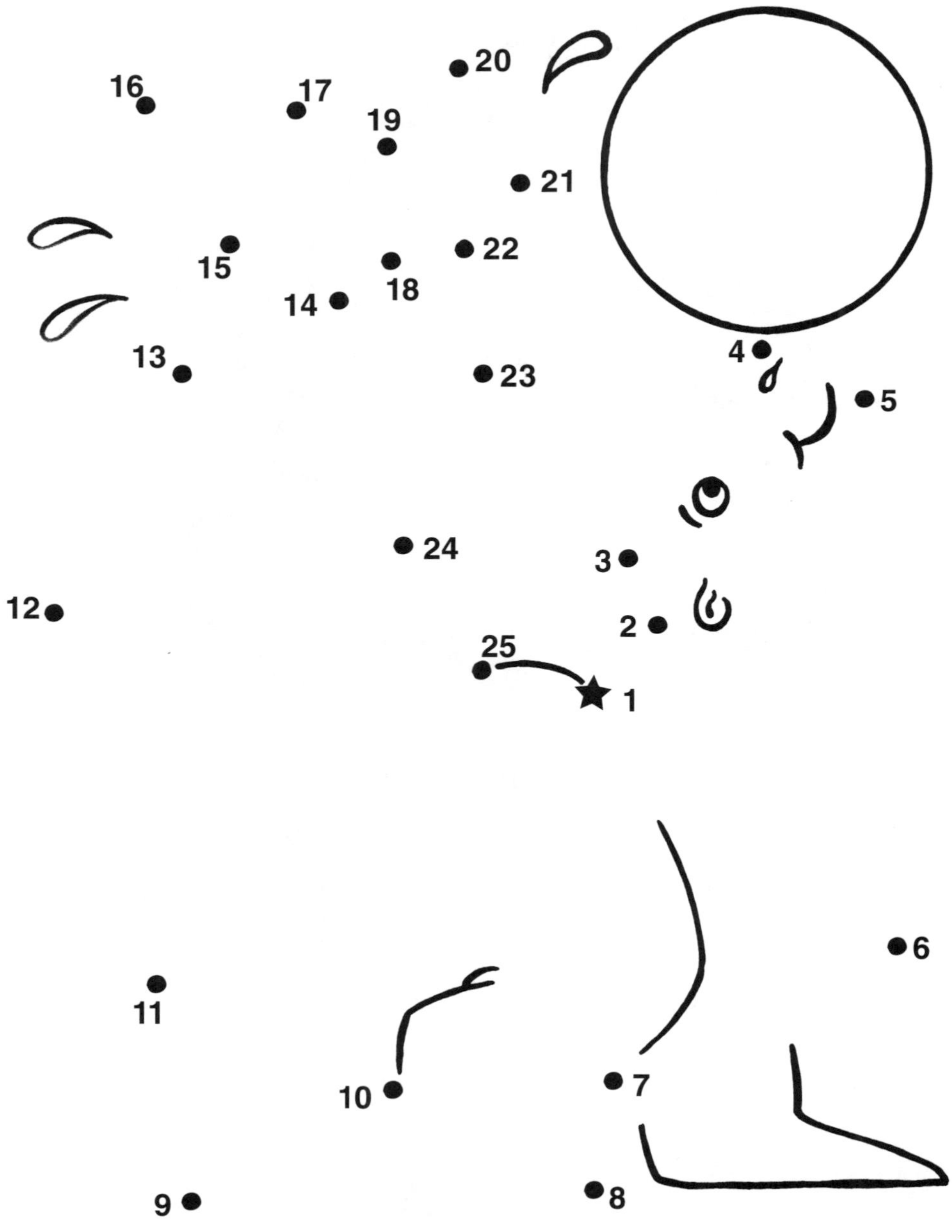

# Tree (1-25)

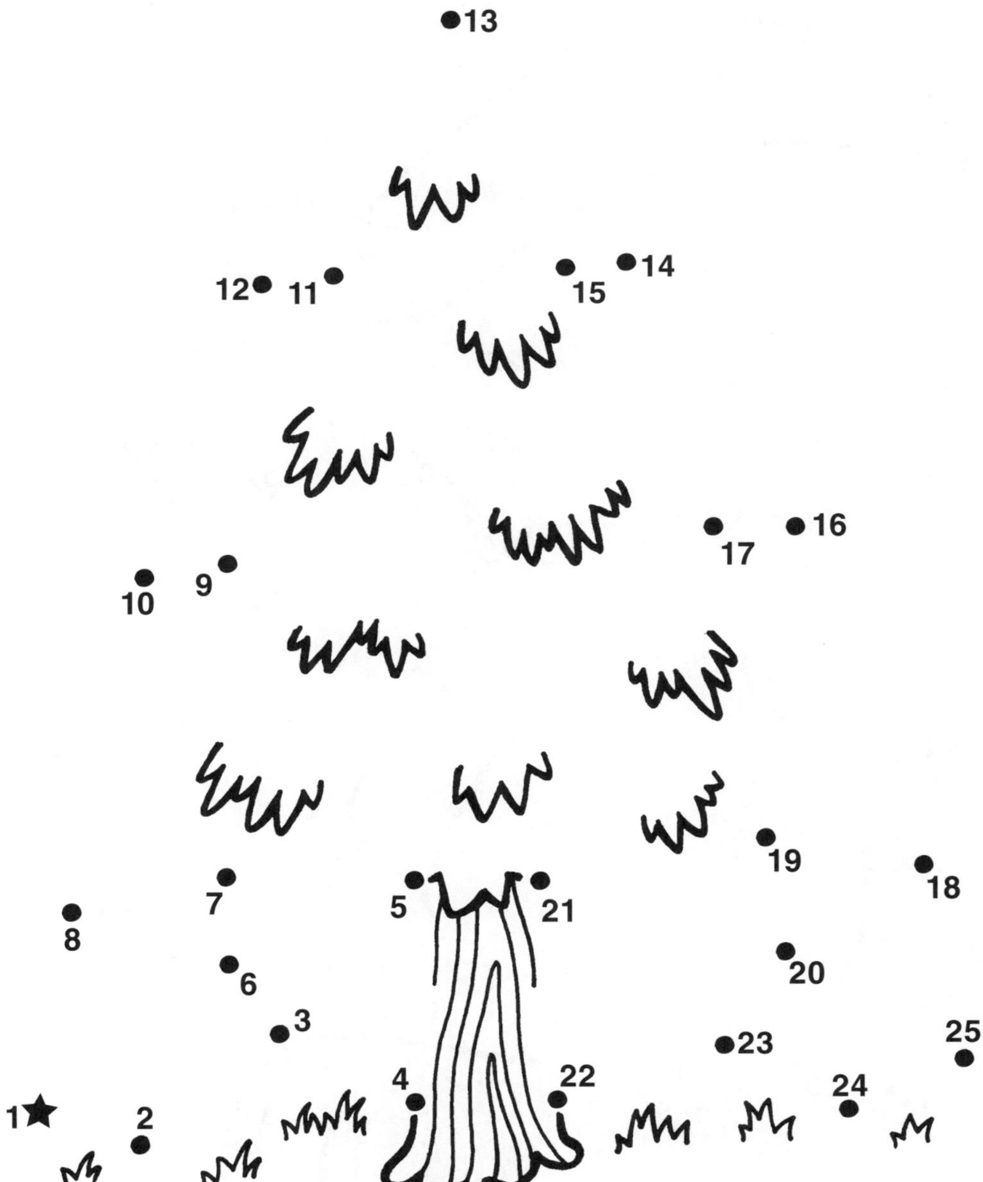

# Rabbit (1-26)

# Best Buddies (1-26)

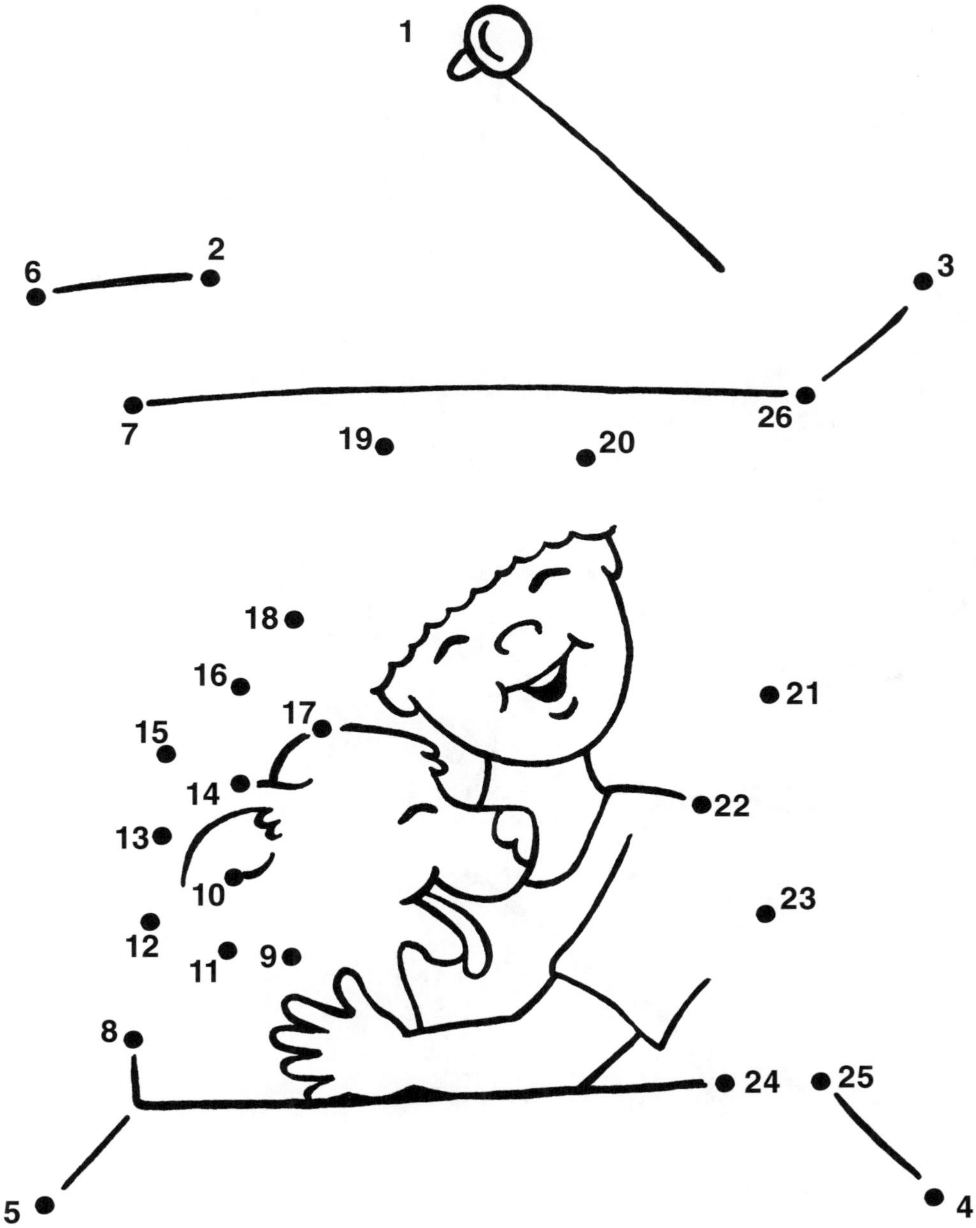

# Ponytail (1-27)

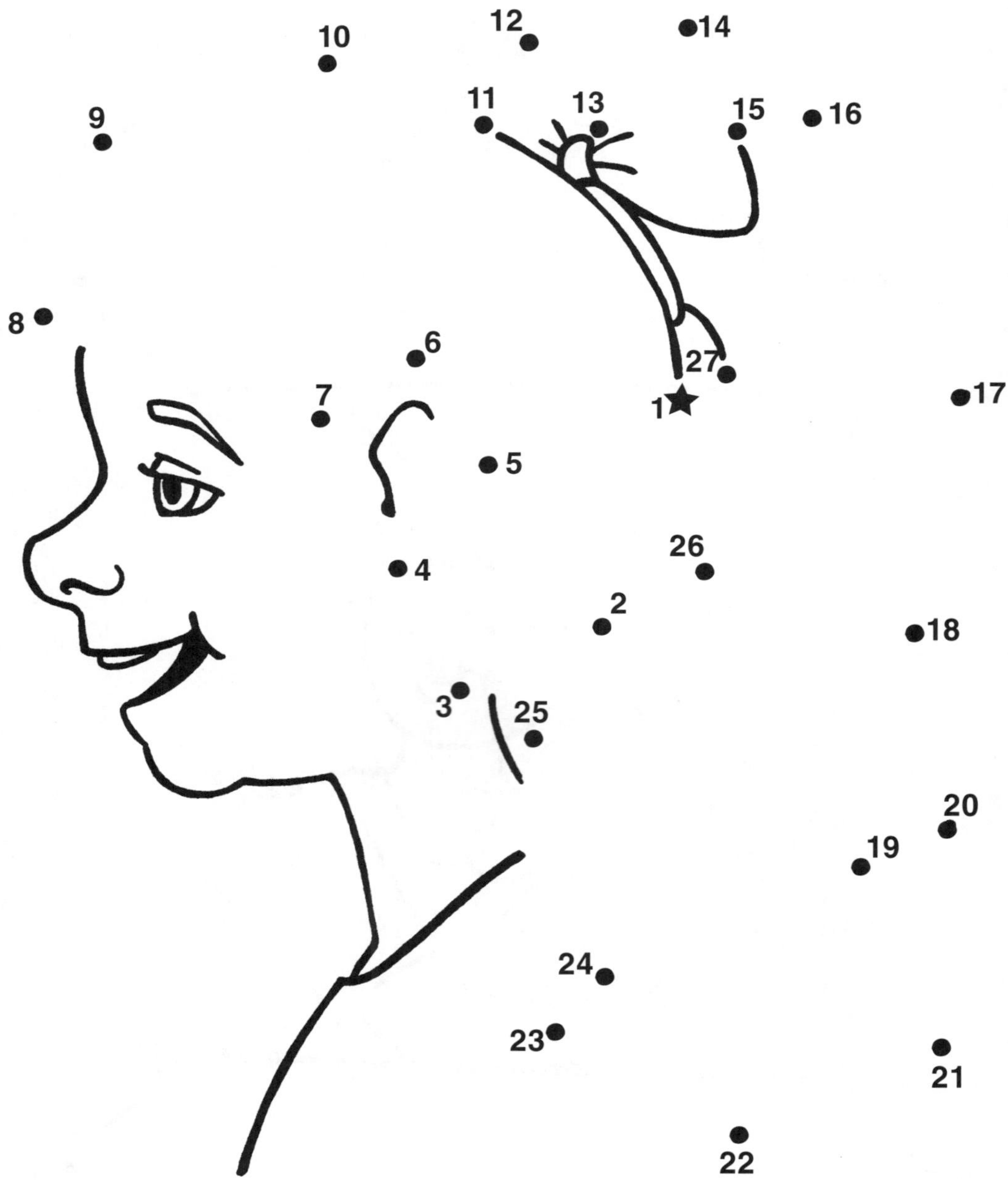

# Shark (1-28)

# Bear and Ball (1-28)

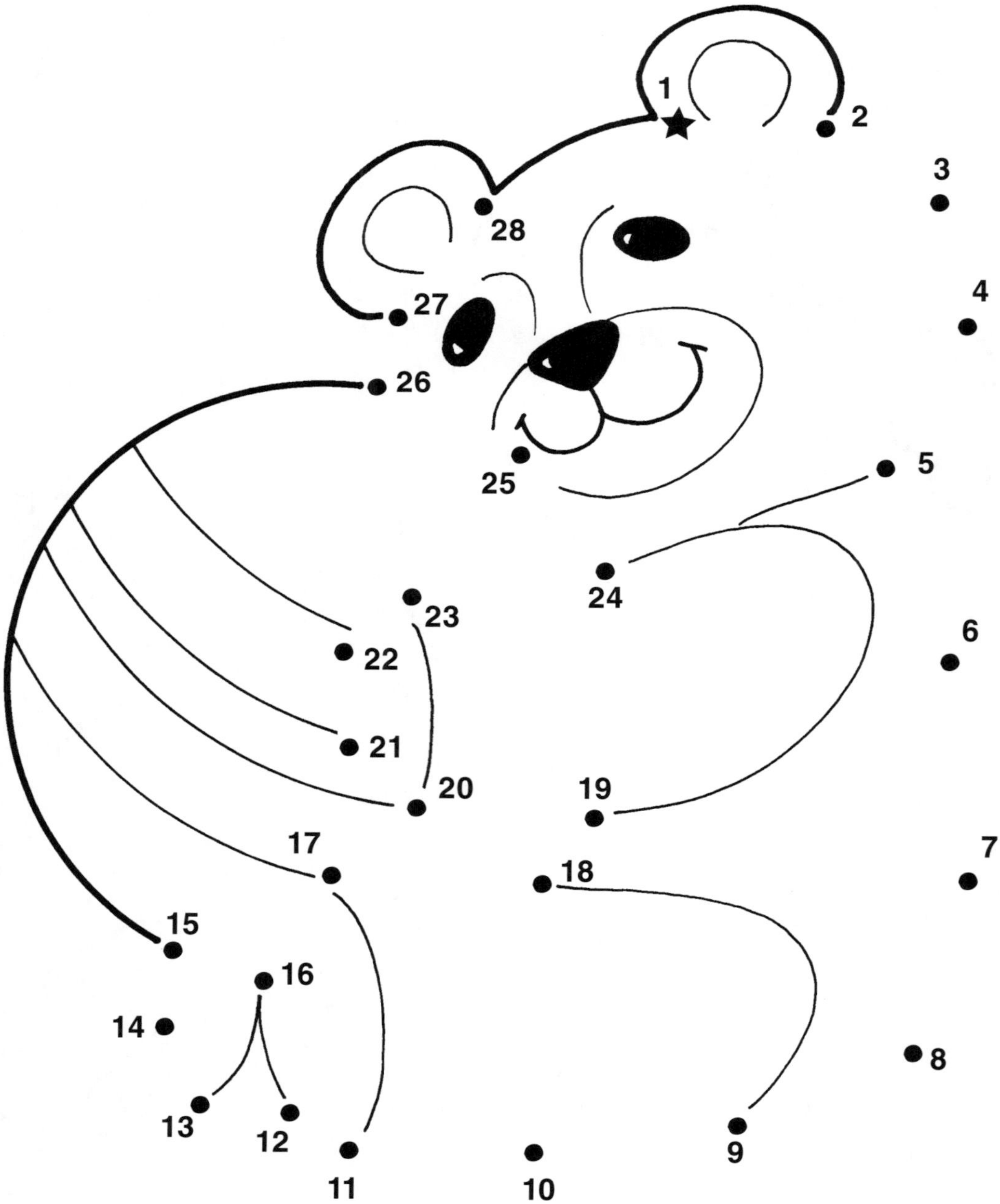

# Mailbox (1-28)

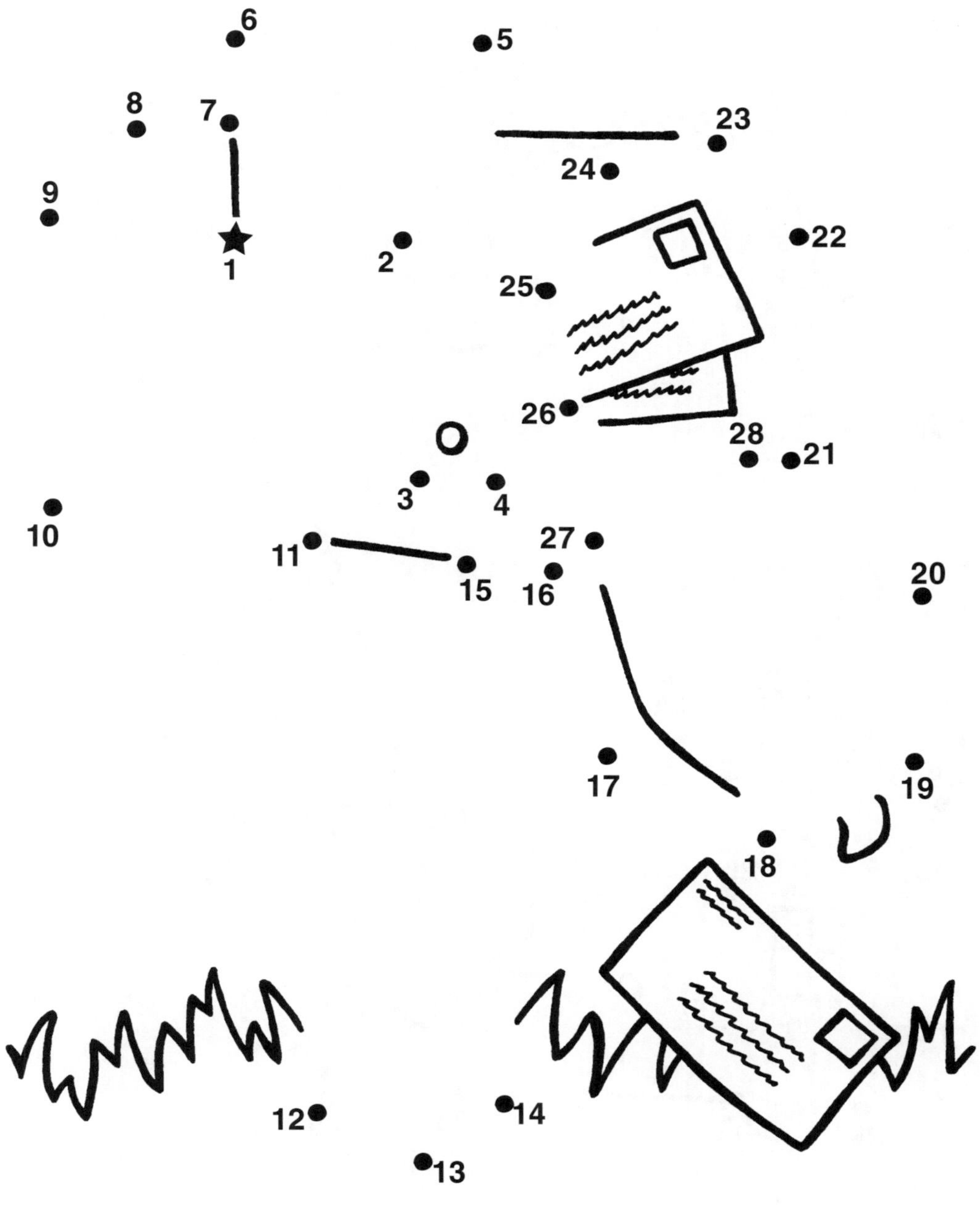

# Mountain Home (1-29)

# At the Beach (1-30)

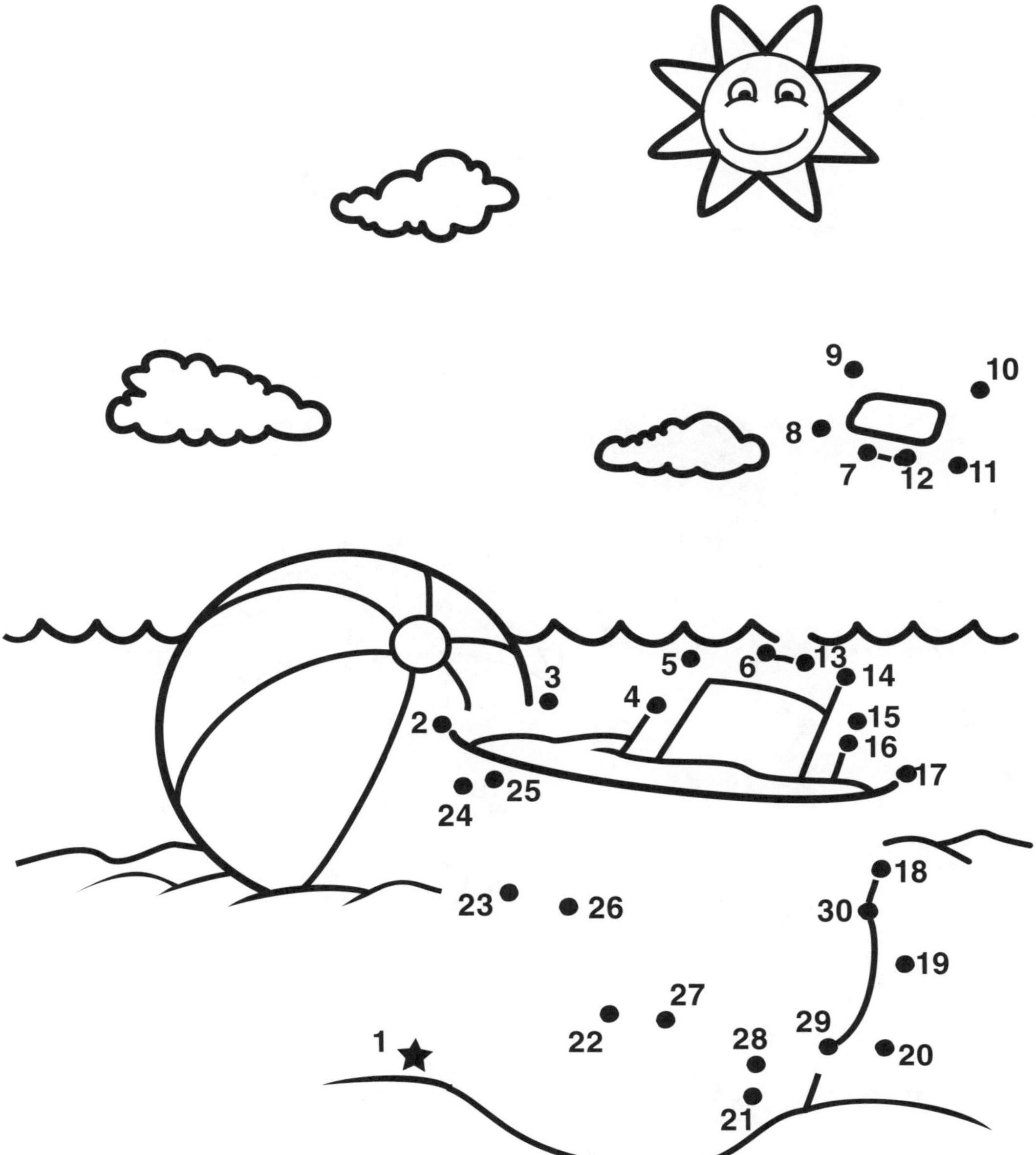

# Space Flight (1-30)

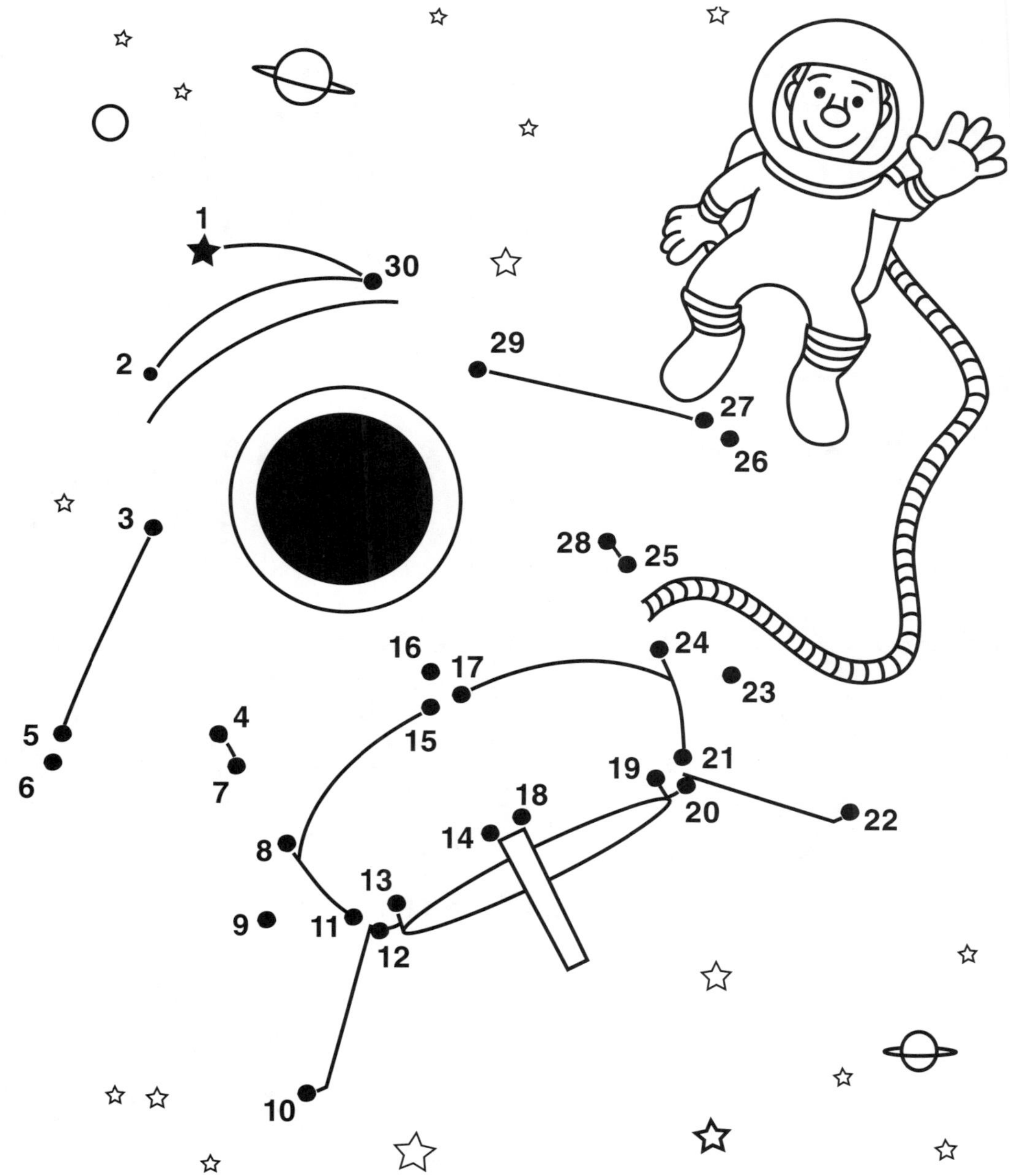

# What Am I? (1-30)

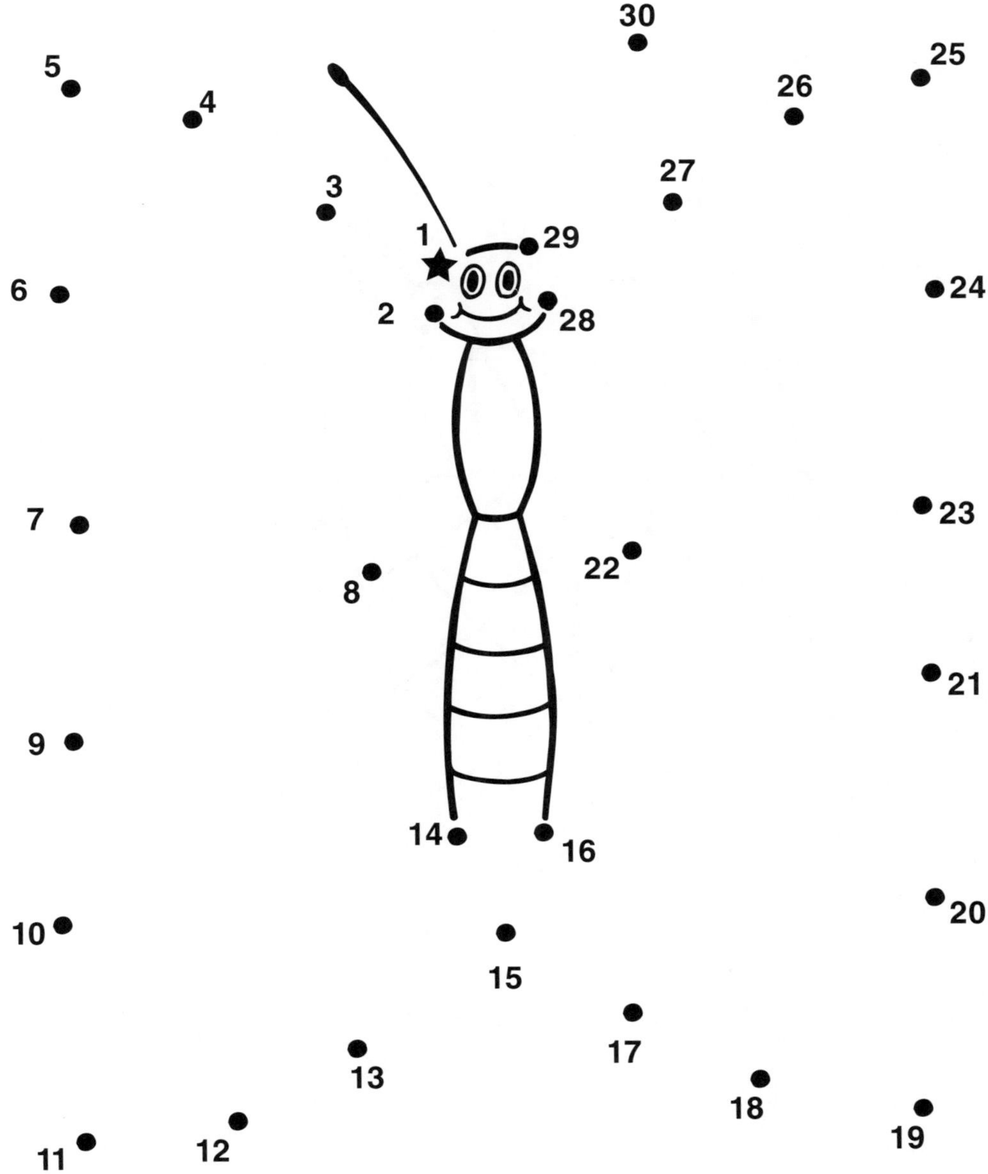
1
2
3
4
5
6
7
8
9
10
11
12
13
14
15
16
17
18
19
20
21
22
23
24
25
26
27
28
29
30

# Pineapple (1-30)

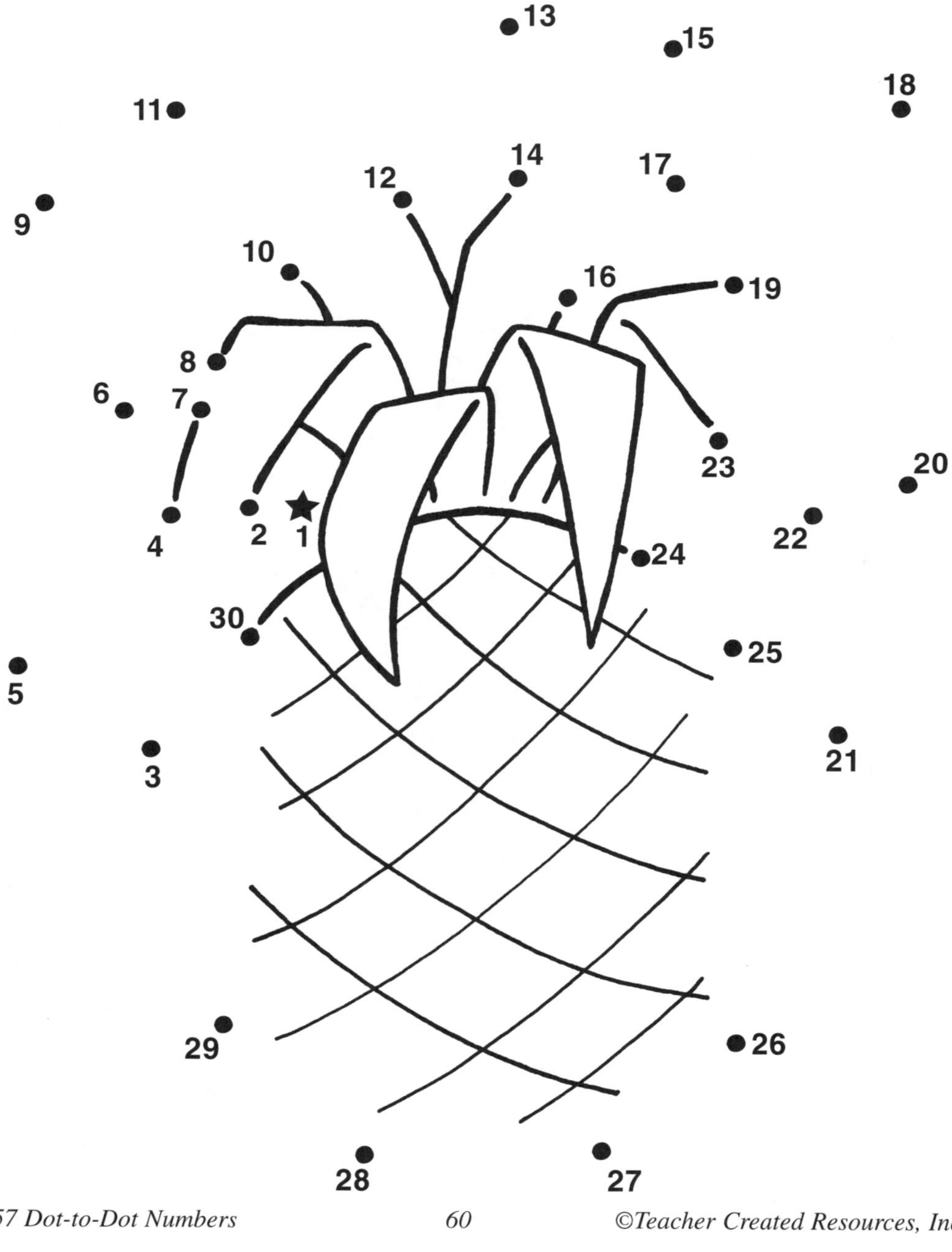

# Under the Sea (1-30)

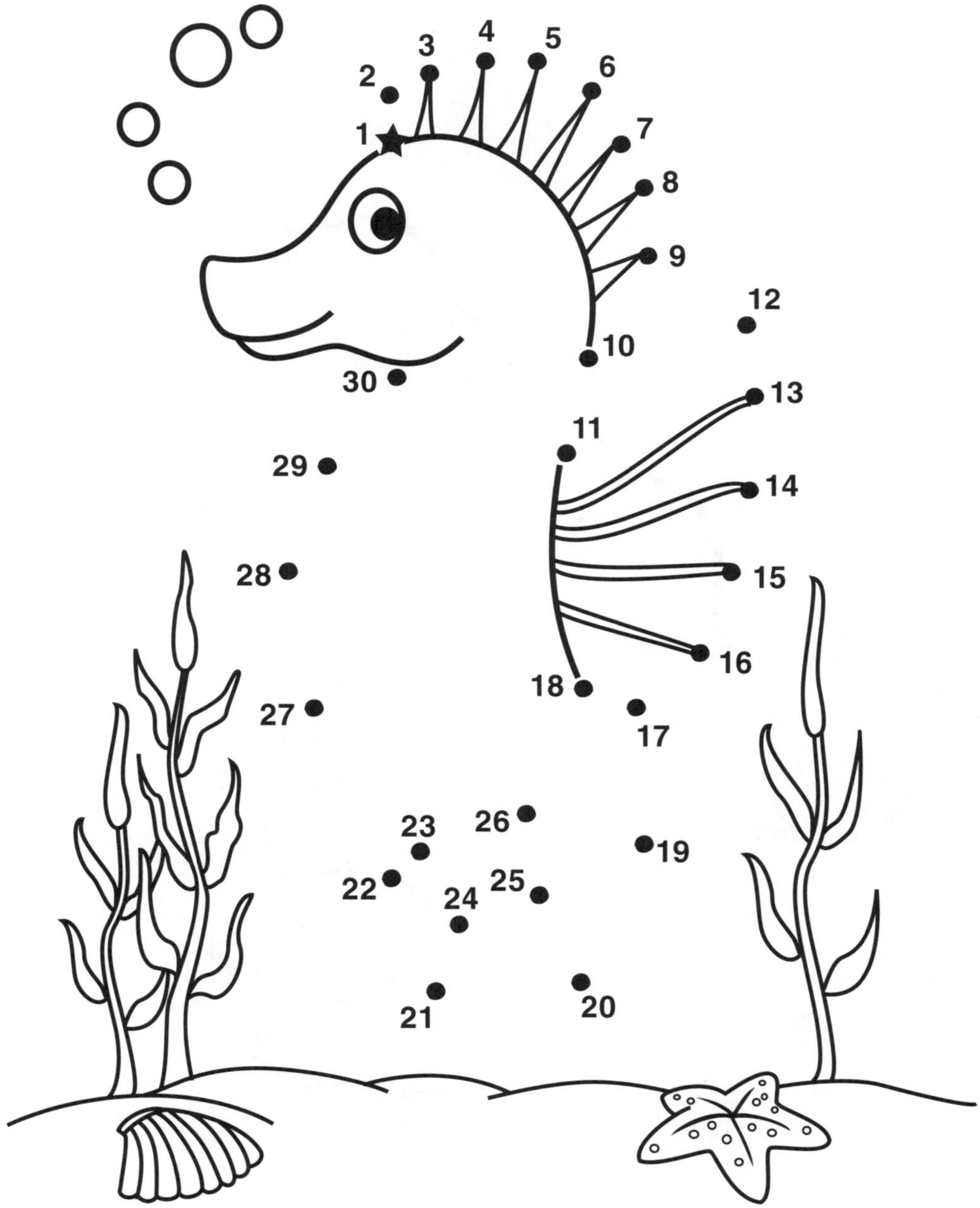

# Dinosaur (1-31)

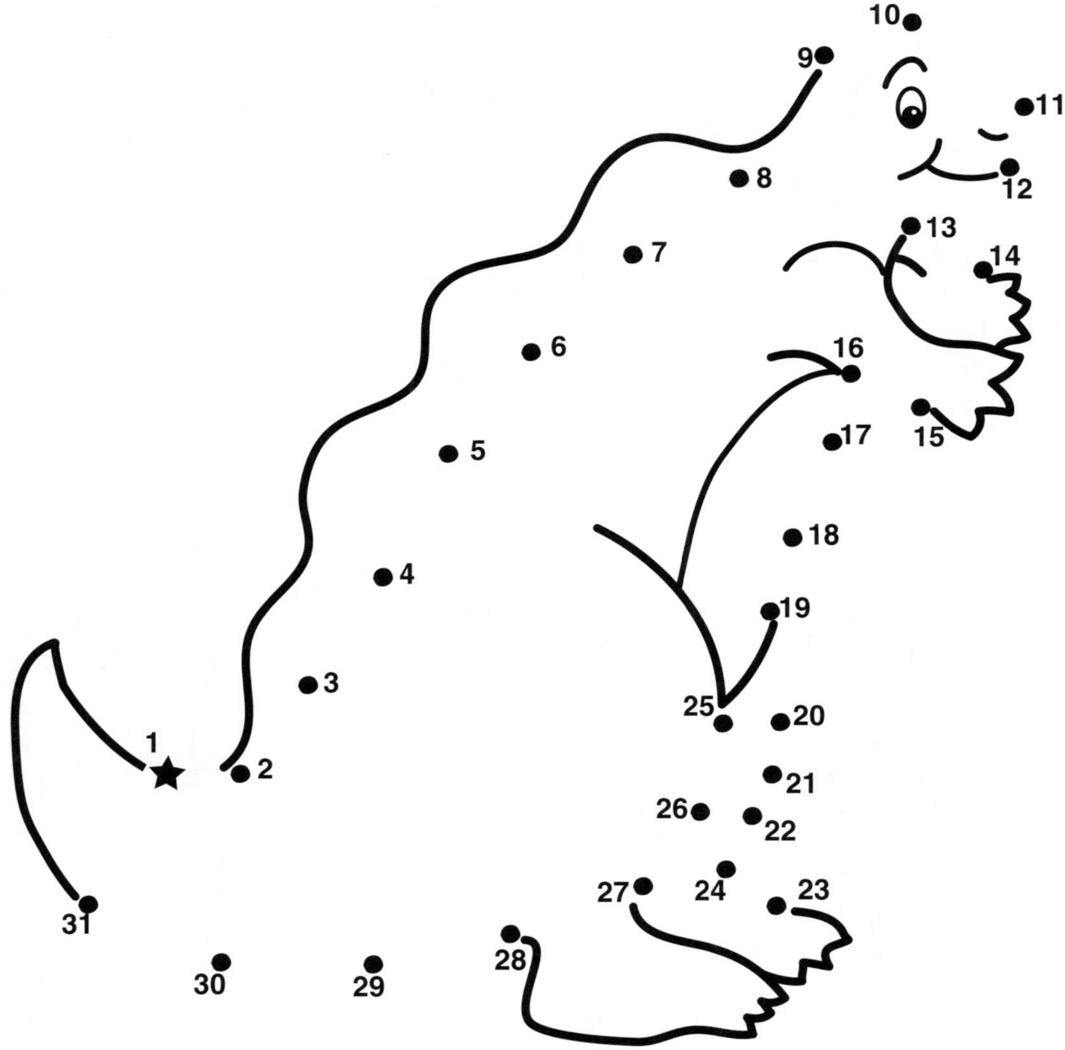

# This Award

# Is Presented To

______________________________

## for

★ Doing Your Best

★ Trying Hard

★ Not Giving Up

★ Making a Great Effort